FLOWERS OF SPEECH

FLOWERS OF SPEECH

*Being Lectures in Words and Forms
in Literature*

by

Sir John Squire

Essay Index Reprint Series

BOOKS FOR LIBRARIES PRESS, INC.
FREEPORT, NEW YORK

First Published 1935
Reprinted 1967

LIBRARY OF CONGRESS CATALOG NUMBER:
67-28769

PRINTED IN THE UNITED STATES OF AMERICA

PREFACE

I SHOULD like to dedicate this book to Mr. Logan Pearsall Smith: he, with Professor Ernest Weekley, the brothers Fowler, the *O.E.D.*, and the late Archbishop Trench, has given me all the fun I have had with words, their meanings and derivations; though I have certainly owed a great deal to much duller, and equally learned, people.

The chapters on the sounds of words are, for what they are worth, my own entirely.

The volume consists of two series of six lectures, each delivered over the "Wireless" in 1930 and 1931. One series was on Words, the other on Literary Forms. I thank the B.B.C. for letting me deliver them; I could not have been certain that anybody ever listened to them had I not had periodical inquiries as to when they were going to be published.

J. C. S.

CONTENTS

PART ONE
The Enjoyment of Words

SHORT BIBLIOGRAPHY

WILLIAM ARCHER: Play-Making. (Chapman & Hall. 7s. 6d.)

GEORGE P. BAKER: Dramatic Technique. (Cape. 18s.)

E. M. FORSTER: Aspects of the Novel. (Arnold. 7s. 6d.)

RONALD FULLER: Literary Craftsmanship and Appreciation. (Allen & Unwin. 8s. 6d.)

H. W. LEGGETT: The Idea in Fiction. (Allen & Unwin. 5s.)

JOHN LIVINGSTON LOWES: Convention and Revolt in Poetry. (Constable. 7s. 6d.)

PERCY LUBBOCK: The Craft of Fiction. (Cape. 3s. 6d.)

ANDRÉ MAUROIS: Aspects of Biography. (Cambridge University Press. 7s. 6d.)

SIR A. QUILLER-COUCH: Shakespeare's Workmanship. (Cambridge University Press. 3s. 6d.)

GEORGE SAINTSBURY: A History of English Criticism. (Blackwood. 12s. 6d.)

SIR LESLIE STEPHEN: Studies of a Biographer. (Duckworth. 4 vols. Readers' Library. 3s. 6d. Vol. I only published so far.)

Tendencies of the Modern Novel. By Hugh Walpole, Luigi Pirandello, D. S. Mirsky, Jakob Wassermann, V. S. Pritchett, Hamish Miles, Erik Mesterton, Milton Waldman. (Allen & Unwin. 3s. 6d.)

PART ONE
THE ENJOYMENT OF WORDS

I

ON WORDS IN GENERAL

I SHOULD like at the outset of this chapter to impress one thing upon readers: that this book is not meant for academic experts, or for persons already versed in the art of writing or familiar with the study of words. For I am no prosodist—I never knew but one practising poet who was—I am no philologist, and, although I must at one time have known some grammar, I have just realized how little I know. Whilst picking up one book after another for the purposes of this little book I came upon a book I had at school. It was *English Prose Composition*, by Marchant and Sergeant (a book which I very strongly recommend to anyone who is willing to take a little trouble to improve his English), and I began reading it. It opens with a brief survey of the elementary principles of syntax. I came upon "Notes on the Predicate," distinctions between compound and complex sentences, and such sentences as "An adverb modifying the complement follows the copula, but if emphatic precedes it," and realized what a world of erudition had faded from my memory.

I remember, I remember
  Those first aspiring years,
The mastery of analysis
  I won with blood and tears;
I could not parse a sentence now,
  Alas! 'tis little joy
To know I'm further off from syntax
  Than when I was a boy.

Yet I doubt if amongst living authors of even the greatest eminence there is one who remembers any more syntax than I do. The lack of an early grounding in grammar usually shows itself later on; but if it has been effectively acquired it can be forgotten when a man's habit of logical expression has been formed, just as a scaffolding is forgotten when a building is complete or a mould broken when the casting has been made. I am here, not as an expert in a language speaking to the experts—whom I may politely ask, at this stage, to switch over to Hilversum or Toulouse —but as a professional writer whose practical business it is to use words as effectively as he can, to listeners whose enjoyment of writing and reading may perhaps be a little intensified by a few conversations on the properties of words, on the objects to be aimed at, and certain faults to be avoided in, their use, and on certain incidental pleasures which may be obtained from the choice and arrangement of them.

I should also add that I shall at times wander from

my syllabus. Nothing, perhaps, could illustrate this
intention more forcibly than a short digression on
the very sentence in which I announced it. "Wander
from my syllabus." Yes, the meaning is clear enough:
but what is there to be observed in the phrase? Well,
to take the last thing first, what an odd word "syllabus"
is! It looks, if you stare at it long enough, almost
comic in an English sentence, so alien is it: and it
certainly would convey no sense of its meaning to
anyone who heard it for the first time. Look it up,
and what do you find? In the first place it shouldn't
be "syllabus" at all. There was a Greek word *sittuba*
which became in Latin *sittyba* (accusative *sittybas*),
which meant the piece of parchment on a book
which bore the book's title in those old ages when
everything was written by hand. The Latin word
appears in Cicero; somebody thought the two "t's"
in a manuscript were two "l's," and in some early
printed editions the two "l's" consequently appeared.
Thus came into existence the alleged Latin word
syllabus, and scholars duly invented a supposed
Greek original, *syllabos*, to account for it. Now had
there been in Greek such a word as *syllabos*, it would
have had something to do with a verb meaning to
put together or collect—the verb from whence we
derive our syllables, which are collections of vowels
and consonants. So, by an easy transition, we reach
our present meaning.

Yet, had I not used that word, what word should I have used? I could hardly say "table of contents," and "the annotated list of the titles of my chapters" would have been much more cumbersome. Probably I should have said "epitome," "synopsis," or "prospectus," all thumping Greek or Latin words. And why? In the answer lies part of the history of England and of civilization, as well as part of the history of language. Our Celtic ancestors had names enough for the things they knew, for natural features and for the common articles of their use: from them we derive words like pool, marl and crag, harness, pony and cart, gown, breeches, button and cradle, bran and—whisky. Our Saxon ancestors supplied us with most of the words we ordinarily use—a child's talk is almost wholly Saxon. But while Celts and Saxons were still living in primitive conditions the nations of the Mediterranean were enjoying an elaborate civilization, and by the time the inhabitants of this island desired words for the operations of scholarship, of theology, and of science, they existed readymade. The more removed from primitive conditions, a thought, or a thing, the more likely it is in English to have a Greek or a Latin name. And an odd thing is that our older importations from the classic languages are often modified in English to such an extent that their origin is effectively disguised, but that later importations, which have come in since education became general, and the mass of the population lost control of the development of the language, tend to remain in or near their original forms. The fight between the two processes, of frigid adaptation and popular development, still goes on. Almost all our new names for mechanical inventions and physical discoveries (not to mention many of the names of our patent medicines) are cold-bloodedly made up from Greek or Latin. It is noticeable that where the words have to be widely used the general public gets at them in the long run. A syllabus is not a thing that the ordinary person has to use every day, so a syllabus it remains. An omnibus is, so it has become a bus. The moving pictures first reached us under the resounding Greek names of cinematograph and kinetoscope. It didn't take long before the general public insisted on using the word "cinema" or the less desirable, because vaguer, "pictures," and the Americans, who still make new native words with a medieval freshness, followed with "movies." "Movies" has not yet come greatly into use here, but its sister, "talkies," has—the reason being that the talking film came to us direct from America with its name, whereas the silent film came to us from France, where the classical tradition of naming things is very strong. Telephone (it means "far-sound" and the Germans call a telephone a "far-speaker") is now generally shortened into "phone," and will ultimately be written as such. "Taxi" had to come: to ask a man to call a taximeter-cabriolet would have been too much. All these words are in common use, and the population has digested the products of learning into ordinary speech. A stethoscope is not a thing in common use; only doctors use it, and the layman sees it seldom, and would be very glad never to see it at all. But if everybody used stethoscopes they would soon become "steths," and in the end the doctors themselves would say "steth"—as, for all I know, they may already amongst themselves. Thus far have we reached, and we could follow the trail indefinitely, from the word "syllabus"; the excursion may illustrate the kind of interest that awaits us if we take to examining the meanings (which usually involves the derivations) of the words that we and other people employ. But in that brief sentence I uttered, "I may wander from my syllabus," there is another noticeable thing if we do but pause to notice it. There is the ghost of a dead metaphor in that "wander."

Had such a phrase never been used before, it would seem very forcible and picturesque: the hearer would see a picture of a man physically sauntering away (down a by-path, perhaps, between hedges) from a disregarded syllabus. But when it sprang so easily to my lips (there, again, is what must have once been a quite vigorous phrase) nothing of the sort was in my mind: I did not realize that there was anything metaphorical about it at all. Yet, had I not used it, I should probably, equally spontaneously and thoughtlessly, have used some other phrase equally embodying a picture and a comparison and equally dim to him who runs and reads. I should have said, let us say, that I would not "adhere" to my syllabus, or that I would not "stick" to it: and neither I nor my readers would have envisaged the grotesque scene which must have been called up by the term long ago when it was fresher. Our common speech is a very museum of such words, and of whole metaphorical phrases, and of similes which are so familiar to us that we do not notice what they mean when we use them. Who thinks of "gold" when he says "As good as gold" —an idiom that must have been very emphatic indeed when it was first coined—or, when he says "As fit as a fiddle," wonders what kind of a fiddle it is that can be thus supremely fit? The translation, "As healthy as a violin," would sound very odd to a Frenchman. Mr. Pearsall Smith, in his fascinating book, *Words and Idioms*, gives long lists of such phrases which are habitually used by us as counters that convey a general meaning whilst their real original meaning is lost. There are what he calls "the doublets," in which two words are habitually used together for the sake of emphasis, such as "enough and to spare," "far and wide," "fear and

trembling," "hammer and tongs," "free and easy,"
"stuff and nonsense," "bag and baggage," "rack and
ruin," "by hook or by crook," "rain or shine," "for
love or money," "through thick and thin." There
are the standard comparisons, such as "as dead as a
doornail," "as dull as ditchwater," "as like as two
peas," "as pleased as Punch," "as stiff as a poker"
—whence we proceed to our innumerable proverbs.
We are, it is often said, very rich in idiom. But the
riches are more often perceived by the foreigner, to
whom all these phrases are new and some bewildering,
than by ourselves, who scatter them about without
realizing how picturesque and apt they are. Our
enjoyment of our language, here again, can be increased if we consider what we say and realize the
wealth of poetry and wit that lies buried in our
ordinary conversation. Even the most "commonplace
type with a stick and a pipe" talks idioms all the
time, simile and metaphors crowding his speech.
Two meet:

A. How goes it?
B. Right as rain.
A. I'm in the pink, too. What's your poison?
B. I'm off it to-day. On the wagon, etc.

There is a history behind every phrase there. I do
not suggest that we should never speak or write
without closely attending to every word. But a habit

of occasional attention may at once lead us to appreciate our treasures of speech more, and, incidentally,
to avoid language of too stereotyped a kind. The
ordinary leading article in a newspaper, though not
so bad as it formerly was, is too often a mere string
of stock phrases which come easily to the pen and
save the fatigue of thought. "You know, etc." And
documents of an entirely mechanical, and much more
artificial, kind are freely to be found elsewhere. In
certain sections of the commercial world counters of
the most detestable kind are used to save the trouble
of accurate thought and speech. From what dim haze
of mind proceeded a letter which I received the other
day from a garage proprietor, and which began:
"*Re* your esteemed favour of 29th ult., same has been
received . . ." How unnecessary that Latin "*re*"!
How mendacious that "esteemed favour," which has
lost all meaning since it came to be applied as a
synonym for any sort of communication, for I had
been refusing to pay a bill, and I am quite sure he
didn't like it. All he meant was, "I have received
your letter. If you don't . . ."

This chapter is a preliminary to others in which
specific and limited subjects will be considered; but
I should like, before we go further, to emphasize in
another way the richness and complexity of civilized
speech in general and English speech in particular.
Let us consider what words are. The primary use of

speech is communication, although someone *did* once say that it was given to us to conceal our thoughts. Where language began we do not know: there is a missing link, in an evolutionary sense, between the grunts of the animals and the first words of man, as there is between the animals and the earliest man biologically. But we can fairly certainly conjecture of what kind the first words must have been. Even to-day we have not lost the faculty of making words by imitating noises: the war gave us words like "whizz-bang" and "crump." The first men made the first words by imitating sounds connected with natural objects, reinforcing their laconic remarks with as much gesture as they could think of. Now suppose we take it that the first word ever thought of for snake was "hiss"—the remains of which are to be found at the beginning of our own words "snake" and "serpent." He would wish to warn somebody that a snake was present; he would say "hiss," presumably point, and then probably run. But centuries may have passed before such simple name words, always multi-plying as an increasing number of types of objects were noticed, were supplemented by the first modi-fications arising from the observation, say, that there were two different kinds of prevalent snake, making rather different noises—and even these would not be made until man had a reason (if only that of curiosity) for remarking on the distinctions. Painful must have been the creation of the elementary words indicating motion and position; slow the growth of the habit of using part of the name of one thing to represent another having some quality in common with it; and long the interval before it dawned on man that he could, when in difficulty, just "give it a name" (as the phrase goes) and get his friends to agree with him, and ultimately infect with his invention neighbours far and wide who may have been wanting a name for just that thing, or who may not have clearly observed the thing until it was shown them with an associated name. There was the great leap. We can now find a name for anything—building it up, on customary principles, out of old roots, or words which, united, will indicate its qualities, or even simply inventing it irrationally. Were a man to invent to-morrow a new and perfect boot-polish and call it "Bombex," we should all (some under protest for a time) call it "Bombex." Were it to supersede all other polishes, in the end the word "bombex" would probably supersede "boot-polish"—and the philologists of the remote future would have one more pretty little problem of derivation to study.

But although we can name anything, our terminology does not, in fact, greatly outrun our needs, and in some regards lags behind them. We often encounter words in foreign languages for which there is no English equivalent. If we wish to convey the sense of one of them, we use the foreign word (if we know it) or have to fall back upon a circumlocution. National habits of thought as well as of life are reflected in national languages; and differences between the thought of one age and that of another are indicated by the appearance of words for things which elsewhere are absent. There is no word in English for "a man who has the same ideas as oneself," though the Esperantists have the word *samideano*. I remember Mr. Pearsall Smith once suggesting that we kill two birds with one stone by calling such a person a "milver," thus providing ourselves with a useful word and the poets with a long-needed rhyme to "silver." The innovation has not yet been made, but suppose that, owing to some new development of social psychology, we found ourselves under the constant obligation of referring to those who share our ideas the word for "a man with the same ideas as oneself" would come soon enough even if it were some cumbersome classic hybrid; and, if convenient, we should evolve another word for "a woman who has the same ideas as oneself." In the Hindustani language, I believe, there are words for all sorts of distant relatives whom we never think of in special categories. There is, as it might be, a word for "the third daughter of my uncle's oldest second cousin on the mother's side." If that be so, it means that certain family relationships are, or were, of more importance in the Hindu social structure than in ours: and words for them were necessary to facilitate not merely speech but thought, which does not move easily in an air of circumlocutions and rough approximations. Naming a thing is part of defining it. As speculation grows and the extension of knowledge, new worlds of words come into existence—words at first sharply confined to their original meanings, then getting (as words will) extended meanings, entering into idioms, acting as the bases of new words and becoming part of the fabric of spoken language, which is an unresting sea.

There are still countless new words awaiting us, not merely for really "new" things, but for things which have been always vaguely present in our consciousness. Anybody who really thinks when he is writing about conveying his whole meaning with the utmost accuracy and concision is sometimes tempted to coin a new word, or "neologism" as it is called. The habit of coining words can be overdone, if the words are ugly or superfluous or not precise in their significance, but it is as well not to be so conservative about it as some people are, for not only do professional writers sometimes need neologisms to express their thoughts, but the general population has always coined spontaneously and better than any single individual when left to itself, and it would be a pity were education to check the inclination or kill the talent. On the other hand, for myself I find the American popular mania for whole dictionaries of new words every year rather tiresome. Language is a live thing which we can help to grow, but it is also an inherited treasury which we ought to reverence. Slang ceases to be amusing when we hear nothing else. It is better not, in one's mere passion for change and facetiousness, to be continually changing the meanings of words, or we lose our hold on the past. As Mr. Arthur Hopkinson says, in his beautiful little book, *Hope*: "Literature in its true forms enshrines words, fixes their meaning, and standardizes their value. The supreme example of this, for the English-speaking race, is found in the Authorized Version of the Bible." It is as well not to try to cramp the passion for creation too much, and we do not want a literary language as well as a popular language. But if some American theorists had their way, the end of it would be that the American population would not be able to read the English Bible without spending years learning Old English in schools, and then no more getting the full flavour out of the words than our own children get out of French words.

II

THE USE OF WORDS

THE ATMOSPHERES AND ASSOCIATIONS OF WORDS

In the last chapter, which dealt with the meaning (which, to some extent, involved the derivation) of words, I asked readers to consider from time to time the words they used, and reflect upon the actual connotations of them. There is a famous character in Molière, M. Jourdain, who discovers that he has been talking prose all his life without knowing it: most English people, in their conversation, scatter idioms, metaphors, similes, paradoxes, wild excesses of the poetic imagination, without knowing it. By periodically pulling ourselves up and examining our own habitual language we may increase our enjoyment of the flavour of our English tongue, and we may learn to avoid outraging that tongue. In this chapter we are going a stage farther: we are considering the flavour of individual words.

I am talking about the associations of words, without reference to the intrinsic pleasantness or unpleasantness of the words themselves. I sometimes meet people—I am going to deal with this question of sound in a subsequent chapter—who suggest that association is everything, that we should think "stomach-ache" a beautiful word if it meant "moonlight," and "Elsinore" an ugly word if it meant "the larger intestine." I don't believe that. I do think that there are such things as words pleasant to the ear and words unpleasant to the ear: associations may temper the harshness of an unpleasantly sounding word or may stop our ears to the beauty of a word. "Keats"—K-E-A-T-S—that is a very harsh-sounding name. When we hear it, so strong is the force of association, we think of nightingales and Grecian urns and autumn, and "that large utterance of the early gods," and Endymion and Hyperion, until, in the end, we think that very coarse and consonantal sound a name which might lull us to sleep. Strip it of its associations, and it is a very unpleasant name: a splutter and a hiss. By the same token many words, very beautiful so far as mere sound is concerned, are lost to us because they have unfortunate associations. Desirous of illustrating this, I thought suddenly of the names of diseases. There we have an extreme instance: call a disease "Oenone" or "Guinevere," and the beauty of the word will be lost, because people will only think of the thing. Yet even between the names of diseases there is a difference made by sound. Can you conceive an Arthurian tale with heroes and heroines called Measles and Mumps? or

a garden of flowers called croup, cramp, and stomach-
ache? Yet listen to this: a poem, in the Pre-Raphaelite
manner (with a slight Shakespearean cross), in which
the names of diseases are used for knights, ladies, and
flowers. If you do not realize from this poem (1) that
some words are more musical than others, and (2) that
association obstructs (as it also assists) our enjoyment
of words, this resounding passage of blank verse will
have been written in vain.

> So forth then rode Sir Erysipelas
> From good Lord Goitre's castle, with the steed
> Loose on the rein; and as he rode he mused
> On knights and ladies dead: Sir Scrofula,
> Sciatica, he of Glanders, and his friend
> Stout Sir Colitis out of Aquitaine,
> And Impetigo, proudest of them all,
> Who lived and died for blind Queen Cholera's sake;
> Anthrax, who dwelt in the enchanted wood
> With those princesses three, tall, pale and dumb,
> And beautiful, whose names were music's self,
> Anaemia, Influenza, Eczema. . . .
> And then once more the incredible dream came back,
> How long ago upon the fabulous shores
> Of far Lumbago, all a summer's day,
> He and the maid Neuralgia, they twain,
> Lay in a flower-crowned mead, and garlands wove,
> Of gout and yellow hydrocephaly,
> Dim palsies, pyorrhoea and the sweet
> Myopia, bluer than the summer sky,
> Agues both white and red, pied common cold,

Cirrhosis, and that wan, faint flower of love
The shepherds call dyspepsia. Gone, all gone:
There came a night he cried "Neuralgia!"
And never a voice to answer. Only rang
O'er cliff and battlement and desolate mere
"Neuralgia!" in the echoes' mockery.

There are some words in the language which have very little flavour and no associations—or so many associations that they cancel one another out. I used a word in that last sentence which will serve as an illustration: the word "the." If it were not a mere article, it might not be a bad word—it goes smoothly, almost swooningly: if there were a thing called "the," it would be possible, when mentioning it, to import something of romance into one's intonation. But there isn't anything called a "the," and that pleasant combination of letters would have to be regarded as sheer waste were it not for the fact that, with an extra "e" and the same pronunciation, we employ it in the most abject and gushing kind of address. Let me fall back upon another word in that sentence: the word "little." That, surely, should be a word divested of accidental implications. After all, everything is either big, little, or middle-sized. But as soon as I look at the word I discover that it means more to me than it obviously sets out to mean. It was a word much employed in a pathetic sense by Shakespeare. Richard II, that most eloquent of minor poets, when

contemplating his latter end, refers to "a little, little
grave, an obscure grave." I cannot pretend that every
time I hear the word "little" pronounced I remember
that passage: on the other hand, I can never be certain
that I do not. Mr. de la Mare, in his beautiful poem,
Farewell, which is a poet's valediction to a world
which he has enjoyed and enriched, says:

> all things we must praise
> Beauty took from those who loved them
> In other days.

There isn't a word, with the possible exception of
the smallest particles, which any of us uses which is
not overlaid by associations. The associations differ
as between class and class, group and group, individual and individual. One sometimes wonders
whether any word which isn't a mere conjunction,
preposition, or interjection means the same thing to
any two people. I am not here referring to the
evident and inevitable differences: as that "love" will
not be quite similarly defined by a man and a woman,
even if they are in love with each other, or "poverty"
mean the same thing to a hard-up millionaire and a
tramp with blistered feet who is sleeping under a
haystack with the rats running over his face. I am
referring to the different atmospheres that words will
have even to two people of the same sex who have
been brought up in similar circumstances. And I am

referring to the different atmospheres that two words which the dictionaries call synonymous will carry with them for the same person.

Let us take an example. An assembly of trees may be called in English by various names: let us select "grove," "wood," and "forest." "Grove" we use very little now. What is the reason? The reason is that it was almost invariably used by Pope and his successors of the eighteenth century to signify any kind of wood or forest. They called young women "nymphs" and young men "swains." They were not quite as artificial as we think them. There were times when they wrote of rural nymphs and rustic swains straying through vernal groves when what they were thinking of was really villagers, male and female, walking in the woods in spring. But it *was* rather a conventional, rather an artificial age, an age that looked at the country through the drawing-room or library window, and the unhappy word "grove" has suffered for it. Put it into a sentence, and the reader at once thinks (1) that you are choosing your words, and (2) that your tastes are rather eighteenth-century.

But leave that word out. Take "wood" and "forest," both of them words in general modern use, and neither of them staled by precious literary usage. A dictionary-maker would be hard put to it to draw a distinction between them: he might say that a wood was a small forest and a forest a large wood. But suppose one had been born in the New Forest, a large part of which is open land covered with brambles and bracken, and had never read any books which interfered with or in any way modified one's notion of a forest, one would think of a forest as a great tract of land, partly covered with trees, partly open; whereas a "wood" to one would be something entirely covered with trees. I wasn't, as it happens, born in the New Forest; but I happen to have browsed pretty freely in the woods and forests of literature. I take myself as an example. What does "wood" mean to me, and what "forest"? When I hear the word "wood" I think of an assembly of trees, not too close together, with sunlight dappling through: oaks and beeches, with primroses in season, and possibly, in glimpses, the antlers of deer—what Shakespeare calls "the Forest of Arden," but I always think of that as a wood. But "forest"! To Shake-speare the words may have meant almost the same thing. To medieval officers of the Crown "forest" meant a wild land (they still officially call Dartmoor a forest) reserved for royal hunting; but to me the word "forest" can never mean what it did to them, for I have read about Russia and the sledges going through forests covered with snow, bells tinkling, and wolves howling; and I have read Hans Andersen and Grimm, and picture at the word endless miles of pines and firs, with smooth, needle-strewn ground underneath, and magician's castles, and lost princesses, and wandering children, and kindly, solitary charcoal-burners; and I have read of the forests of the Amazon and the Congo—dank, marshy wildernesses, full of strange butterflies, and steam, and crawling rivers. In me, as it happens, the fairy-tale is uppermost: utter that word to me, and that is what I see, or, if I don't see it, it is at the back of my mind, intertwining with the picture that I *do* see. The word always gives me a little thrill, even when they announce that song called *Down in the Forest Something Stirred*. That thrill I probably have in common with hundreds of thousands of English people who have had the same sort of training and background; it must be missed (except what of it may spring from the mere hushed and evocative sound of the word) by everybody who has not.

Now, why all this long discursion upon two words? Well, for this simple reason: whatever is true of "wood" and "forest" is true of almost every substantive we use. There are bounds of narrative and statement beyond which we cannot go. The Roman Catullus, hopelessly in love with a repulsive and fascinating coquette, writes, *"Odi et amo."* It translates straight into "I hate and love," and it is forcible enough to make an impression in any tongue. Get beyond this plain sort of statement, and the man of letters is appealing and trading upon, if you like, associations which he shares, or hopes he shares, with his readers, and the associations may spring either from literature or from life. The moment the bare statement is qualified or compared, we are being "got at."

Take almost any celebrated passage of poetry, not directly dramatic, which moves you—you don't know why—and examine it: you will find that every word is pregnant with associations whose power over you the poet, either with deliberate cunning or through sheer force of natural genius, has exploited. Take Wordsworth's *Highland Reaper*. She sang

> Of old, unhappy, far-off things
> And battles long ago.

What was she actually singing about? I don't know: possibly Flodden. But observe how Wordsworth, with his "old," his "unhappy," his "far-off," his "long ago," touches every stop of the pathetic organ, reminding us not only of our own lost past, lost childhood, lost pain, lost happiness, not only of the passage of time and the imminence of death and the mystery of the hereafter, but of all the works of older authors than he, in which "long ago" rang out as a sad memorial chime: and since *he* newly consecrated those words they have an even fuller force than they had before him. The very rose and nightingale, though the first was the most delicate and richest of flowers, and the second a bird that sang sweetly at night, were never what they are when a thousand poets have associated them with all that is freshest and tenderest in our hearts—as the cheap bards well know who get half the way by merely mentioning them.

That was a simple passage. Take an equally well-known but far more artificially composed one, Keats's

Magic casements opening on the foam
Of perilous seas in faery lands forlorn.

I think it possible that this passage has been over-rated: it contains so many exquisitely "poetical" words, quintessentially romantic. But there is no doubt that—quite apart from the merits of sound, and we are considering sound in a later chapter—the poet exploits association in these lines to the utter-most. There are all kinds of subtle touches that make their effect. The "foam," with its visual image of the sea's edge, suggests all that lies behind the wave that makes the foam; the plural "seas" has something of the illimitable about it, which the singular "a perilous sea" would not have had. But examine the other words. "Magic" is obvious in its other-worldliness, and "faery" is but a repetition of it, bringing a sug-gestion, none the less there because we do not realize it, of all the dreamlands to which changelings and

vagrant poets were snatched away in the old ballads
—the spelling reinforcing this. "Casements" is fairy-
tale and antique again. "Windows" would have conveyed the dull surface meaning, but that word, in
Keats's day as in ours, would have carried with it a
suggestion of Georgian brick and sashes; "casements,"
though not an entirely dead word, suggested small
panes, bygone ages, ivy leaves, maidens leaning out.
"Forlorn," to a brutal realist, would appear to add
little to the passage: literally, I suppose, it would
suggest that there used to be fairies in the place, but
that they had now deserted it. Keats was not thinking
of literalness or of fairies present or absent: he was
trying to reinforce by an epithet an impression of
strangeness and remoteness; and he hit on a word
which was the very essence, after a long history in
literature, of unaccountable loneliness, and which had
been rhymed a thousand times to the "horn" which,
coming from some mysterious quarter, rang through
the solitudes, and faded.

No two people have quite the same associations.
All people have some associations in common: the
works that are most universally appreciated and about
which there is least dispute among people of taste are
those which deal with these. The moment adjectives
come in, differences of taste become evident. These
are not only accountable for, as is generally assumed,
by differences in ear and moral sensibility, but by

actual differences in what is called "reference." An Assyrian might have written, and have languished and luxuriated as he wrote:

Sweet as the face of Asshur-Bani-Pal.

To us, who know nothing of Asshur-Bani-Pal's face, it is a statement and no more, though we may take the gentleman's judgment for granted. Let Burns say, "My love is like the red, red rose," and we know what he means, and what he means is not literal.

I suggest that readers might amuse and instruct themselves by taking some of their favourite passages in literature and saying to themselves: "Why (over and above any straight emotional or moral appeal) does this passage appeal to me so much? What underlies the words? How far am I being moved by incidental associations, and how far did the author set out to move me thus?" Along this path is to be found a secondary means of enjoying literature, and, I may add, new wonderment at the skill of the great writers, who do not delete and delete, and substitute and substitute, without good reason, and whose good reason is very often the desirability of taking the reader in flank by associations, as well as in front by assertions.

III

THE MUSIC OF WORDS

In the last chapter there was a short romantic poem in which knights, ladies, flowers, and faery lands all bore the names of diseases. It was meant to illustrate how our views of the sound of words are modified by their associations: intrinsically ugly words have their ugliness concealed—the name "Keats," for example, conjures up the images of moons and nightingales and cool evening woods—and intrinsically beautiful words have such unbeautiful associations that we never realize how beautiful they are. If those medical terms, embodied in the setting I gave them, sound musical when spoken or read aloud, the collateral point is effectively made—that some words are more pleasing to our ears than others, quite apart from their meaning. This is, or ought to be, a commonplace: but one does occasionally meet tiresome people who try to maintain that *everything* depends upon associations. They usually quote, "What's in a name? A rose by any name would smell as sweet." Even that remark of Shakespeare's *may* not be wholly true as it stands: our very enjoyment of the scents of plants may to some extent be magnified or diminished by the music, or lack of it, in their names; verbena, in that regard, may have an advantage over annual stock or tobacco-plant. But Shakespeare never said that a rose by any other name would sound as agreeable: no one ever had a more sensitive ear than he, and he might never have mentioned the flower, smell it ever so sweetly, had it been called Trublosch or Swixswix. There is a good deal in the mere sound of names. We recognize this, of course, when we are talking of languages: we say that Italian is the tenderest of languages and that German is the harshest: we sometimes console ourselves with the reflection that English, with its mixture of strong Teutonic words and flowing Latin ones, can command a greater range of music than any other tongue. When people quote what they believe to be "perfect" single lines, the lines will usually be found to be lines embodying sublime thought or feeling in words which flow effortlessly from the tongue, like

> Sunt lachrymae rerum et mentem mortalia tangunt

and

> In sua voluntade e nostra pace.

Even the sublimest thought would not be quoted as an example of a perfect line (at any rate in this country) if it were expressed in such words as

> Schloggel brisks kikpok peff gogwolduk skump.

Those, I hasten to add, are not words from any known language—or, at any rate, from any language known to me. No human voice, I think, could make them affecting or melodious. The poet Coleridge—you will find some examples in the Oxford edition of his works—used to write down nonsense verses in order to record melodies; Lewis Carroll, in several of his poems, moves us because of the very music of his syllables, by sentences which mean little more than Coleridge's. No effort of mine could make that very dental spluttering that I have just recited musical. I will try. In the reign of Charles II a French traveller came to England, and noticed, as one of the oddest things about it, that the English had a curious way of reciting their poetry in a melancholy, dreamy croon. I will try it on that line. It ran, you will (or will not) remember:

Schloggel brisks kikpok peff gogwolduk skump.

Listen: I will do my best in the other-worldly way:

Schloggel brisks kikpok peff gogwolduk skump.

Do what I may, I cannot avoid clickings which are unpleasing to the ear, and contortions of the mouth —resulting from difficult gradations from one consonant to another—which produce the effect of painful effort and not of ease. It's absurd, of course: it sounds like a drunkenness test. And that, of course, suggests the thought: what is difficult to say is not pleasant to hear.

Now I am far from suggesting that the harsh-sounding words and conjunctions of words have not their uses. If you want to convey the notion of a smash, you could not have a better word than "smash"; if you wish to convey the notion of a smack and a bang, you could not make better words than "smack" and "bang." The English language—as I remarked in my first chapter—is full of these onomatopoeic, imitation words, and the harsh and startling word fits the harsh and startling thing. Our language is very imitative, and our poets have made good use of it. Consider the effect that sound plays in the conveyance of the meanings of "a crack of thunder," "a peal of thunder," "a roll of thunder," "a rumble of thunder," and "a distant muttering of thunder"—all common phrases, and all attempting to indicate, by sound as well as by the definitions and associations of the words, the qualities of the first impacts of the noise as well as of the later, prolonged, awful, majestic reverberations. Naturally, if the sound is rough or unpleasant, the word should be—the closer words fit things the better; as I remarked before, it is a pity that exquisite, languishing words should be wasted upon disgusting ailments. The Italians, with their language full of liquid words which end in vowels, find it difficult to represent a rough noise. Tennyson endeavoured to convey the clattering tumult of a battle of men in armour with the refrain, "Clang battle-axe and clash brand." You have only to change that into the sham Italian "Clanga battle-axa and clasha brando," and you will see what I mean. The difficulty for the Germans—though Heine, among others, triumphantly overcame it—is to produce a soft effect in a language full of rough gutturals and dentals and emphatic sibilants. Writing is a mode of speech: we hear what we see in print! at any rate we lose a great deal if we don't hear it.

But when we talk of the music of words we usually think of pleasant sounds, not of representations, however accurate, of unpleasant sounds in nature. Music in this sense resides in single words; in the placing of words together; and in the general arrangement and flow of a number of words in sentence, paragraph, or stanza. "Endymion," "tenderly," "moon," "lonely," "eternity"—like the "myopia" to which I referred before—are essentially melodious words. I suppose that analysis, in the last resort, would discover that our preference for these is very deep-rooted. Birds usually make two kinds of noises: they have their "songs" and their "alarm-cries," and the latter are very much more sharply consonantal than the former. Words like "purr" and "coo" indicate pleasure and comfort in human beings as well as in cat and dove: "shriek" and "scream" are quite different matters. All pleasant and beautiful things are best represented by words in which the consonants are not too acute and the vowels are soothingly drawn out. Whatever may be at the bottom of it, the fact remains that we do prefer certain words to others for sound, and that is a thing that every writer has to bear in mind.

And the moment words are juxtaposed the thing becomes more evident still. Unless there is a positive reason for not giving us pleasant, flowing sound, a man should aim at giving it; or he produces a less powerful effect than he might. Lines in poetry, though they may technically "scan," may be so overcrowded with consonants that fight one another, or vowels that involve a continual, ungraduated changing on the mouth that they cannot be spoken musically, and produce an effect of congestion and strain. Browning is full of such lines. Take the often-quoted couplet from the poem which ends "What porridge had John Keats?":

> Nokes hints blue, straight he turtle eats,
> Stokes prints blue, claret crowns his cup.

The lips, tongue, and teeth have heavy work getting it out; and when it comes out it sounds like a mixture of hissing and chattering. It would be well enough were it done intentionally, but it is not. Browning,

after his first youth, was so preoccupied with his
meaning that he forgot all about music. Nobody
would suggest that the plain, matter-of-fact observations in these two lines demand or justify any particular loveliness of lilt: but there is no reason why
harsh, cacophonous lines should be thrown at us
wantonly. When Browning was more in vogue than
he is now—the best of him must return—it was his
habit of clotting consonants together and awkward
transitions of vowels that the parodists chiefly fastened
upon, and what parodists fasten upon are usually
weaknesses.

Melody may be secured by a careful vigilance over
the contacts of words and by a careful (though with
most good writers the melody comes naturally, if
at all) watch over sequences of consonants and
vowels. R. L. Stevenson, who thought more about
this matter than most men, once stated that the
sequence of "p," "f," and "v" was very effective; as
it might be in "passed to a farther vale." Here there
is a gradation from the softly explosive "p," through
"f," which is half-way, to "v," which is the softest
and least consonantal consonant that there is. Why
should that sequence please us? For one thing,
because it costs us little effort to proceed from the
pronunciation of one of these letters to that of the
next: the lip movements are very similar. For another,
the sequence grows softer as it goes on. You may

remember in Shakespeare how, after music has been played, an enchanted hearer says, "It has a dying fall." A dying fall pleases us as much in words as in wordless tunes, and it will often be found that it is in the presence of "a dying fall" that resides the power of a passage of poetry or prose to move us— the melody of the sigh.

In the music of words we can find parallels to all the music of the composers, from the simple folk-song to the elaborate symphonic construction. Simple, sweet melody flowed from the lips of the old ballad-writers—and more consciously on occasion from Shakespeare. In Shakespeare's more elaborate fine passages, as in the great passages of the English Bible, and the seventeenth-century prose masters, and Ruskin, and Pater, we find an elaborate building-up with a view to musical effect. Take the hackneyed passage from the *Tempest*:

> These our actors,
> As I foretold you, were all spirits, and
> Are melted into air, into thin air;
> And like the baseless fabric of this vision,
> The cloud-capped towers, the gorgeous palaces,
> The solemn temples, the great globe itself,
> Yea, all which it inherit, shall dissolve,
> And, like this insubstantial pageant faded,
> Leave not a rack behind. We are such stuff
> As dreams are made on, and our little life
> Is rounded with a sleep.

Or take this passage from the late Lord Balfour:

> We survey the past, and see that its history is of
> blood and tears, of helpless blundering, of wild
> revolt, of stupid acquiescence, of empty aspirations.
> We sound the future, and learn that after a period,
> long compared with the individual life, but short
> indeed compared with the divisions of time open to
> our investigation, the energies of our system will
> decay, the glory of the sun will be dimmed, and the
> earth, tideless and inert, will no longer tolerate the
> race which has for a moment disturbed its solitude.
> Man will go down into the pit, and all his thoughts
> will perish. The uneasy consciousness, which in this
> obscure corner has for a brief space broken the
> contented silence of the universe, will be at rest.
> Matter will know itself no longer. "Imperishable
> monuments" and "immortal deeds," death itself, and
> love stronger than death, will be as though they had
> never been. Nor will anything that *is* be better or
> be worse for all that the labour, genius, devotion,
> and suffering of man have striven through countless
> generations to effect.

Or take, in its harder and coarser way, almost any of
the more eloquent paragraphs of Macaulay. You will
find, if you read them naturally, letting yourself go
where the meaning and the cunning arrangement of
alliterations and repetitions stresses, of short or prolonged sentences, closely joined or widely separated
pauses, take you, that the passages are as clearly
marked for interpretation by the vocal instrument as

any page of music—you simply cannot help the crescendos and rallentandos and lentos and staccatos —the passages rise and roar and dwindle into peace, the voice swells and sinks again, and the impression which the writer wished to make by what, bluntly, he said, has been reinforced by the way in which he said it. That most of the finest passages, musically, in English echo the cadences of the Authorized Version, and have a bearing on mortality, is another matter: there may be a touch of the mystery of our birth and death about all the art that moves us.

The least of us can take some trouble about the sound of our sentences, and can gain in the power of persuasion by the reinforcement of meaning by sound which conveys a part of meaning. "Hist!" which has unhappily died out, was far more effective than "I say, what was that?" But there is one point more which I must make before I end a chapter which can do no more than touch the fringe of a vast subject. Some cynic once observed: "Take care of the sounds and the sense will take care of itself." That was going too far. For a completely satisfactory effect, the garment of melody must fit closely to the body of meaning; and in all the masterpieces it does. But a writer who gets too preoccupied with sound for its own sake tends to end with no effect but the effect of sound: some of Shelley and most of Swinburne suffers from this drawback. It is a mistake to produce

a melody so overpowering, so unrelated to the
fluctuating meaning of the words within that the
reader or listener forgets the meaning in the sheer
sensuous enjoyment of the music. It is a commonplace
that much of Swinburne's inferior work suffers from
this defect; but even some of his best work is ham-
pered by it. Take, out of that famous and wonderful
chorus from *Atalanta*, the stanza:

> Where shall we find her, how shall we sing to her,
>   Fold our hands round her knees, and cling?
> O that man's heart were as fire and could spring to her,
>   Fire, or the strength of the streams that spring!
> For the stars and the winds are unto her
> As raiment, as songs of the harp-player;
> For the risen stars and the fallen cling to her,
>   And the south-west wind and the west wind sing.

I have, I suppose, read that a hundred times, but I
dare not swear that I have ever noticed the details of
the statements made: I am carried away by the
intoxication of the chant; the poet raves and croons,
his eyes sparkle, his hair flows in the wind, and I
hear only the noise he makes, and never notice the
things, very likely interesting, which he is saying.
This defect, of an actual overplus of melody, is
uncommon in modern prose-writers, but even in
prose it is evident in the great sermonizers of the
Jacobean and Caroline ages: whatever they say "hath
a dying fall," and one tends to listen swooningly to

them, without being aware whether they are describing the flowers of spring or warning us .against our latter end.

I would suggest to readers that they should turn to passages which have moved them, and examine how far, in some, the weight of the meaning has been reinforced by music, it may be, cunning and calculated, and how far, in others, the magic of verbal melody may have screened from them the actual literal meaning of the author.

IV

THE PECULIAR PROPERTIES OF POETRY

PERHAPS instead of "The Peculiar Properties of Poetry," I ought to have said "The Peculiar Properties of Verse." For the other phrase at once provokes the question: What is Poetry? and to that question there have been a thousand answers, none of them comprehensive enough to win general assent. The word is sometimes used in a narrower sense of literature written in metrical form; or, in a still narrower sense, of good literature written in metrical form. But it is also used, very often by the same people who sometimes assume the other connotation, of any form of writing or even speech, in which a heightened state of emotion is expressed in language which communicates it. I have known men of whom people commonly said that they were "born poets," although they had never written a line of verse, or even of prose, which was intended to be literature. And the exclamation: "That is sheer poetry!" is a common one on our lips, when we encounter in conversation, in the speeches of politicians, in the addresses, sometimes, of counsel, and in almost all the great prose works of the world, passages which exalt us by their combination of affecting sound and lofty or tender sentiment. Think of any definition of poetry that you have ever heard, and you will find it inadequate. Wordsworth said it was "emotion recollected in tranquillity"—a valuable contribution to criticism, but a remark that has no bearing on the differences between verse and prose. Lord Byron, who wrote at white-heat, said that it was the flow of lava, to which, were it suppressed, the alternative would be an earthquake: there is not much question of tranquillity there, and once more the question of verse, of regularity of rhythm, and of beat, does not come in.

Where so many have failed, I am not going to rush in. But perhaps one image and one observation may help. Nobody denies—even in this questioning age nobody has yet been found to deny—that there is a difference between day and night. But who can say precisely when day ends and night begins, when night ends and day begins? There is, at dawn and dusk, a period of transition, of perfectly continuous modification, during which there is no precise moment at which we can say that here it is definitely night and here it is definitely day. In the same way poetry, in the broadest sense, and prose fade into each other. Nobody disputes that Bradshaw's time-table is prose, or that Milton is poetry: but there are all sorts of gradations between. After generations of discussion —and people always grow hottest in discussions which are certain to have no conclusion—we may most comfortably reconcile ourselves to the opinion that an exact definition is impossible.

The observation I would couple with this image is that where prose becomes emotional it does tend towards the condition of verse. It tempts the reader to chant it: there is a propensity in it towards repetition of stress and cadence and equal length of phrase: towards pattern, in short. Any crowd, primitive or civilized, in a state of excitement tends to work off its feelings in regular, rhythmical noises—beats of tom-tom, clappings of hands, stampings of feet. And I think that in all prose, conventionally so-called, which rises to a high pitch of emotion or imagination, we find—if we take careful note—that we are approaching verse. The whole range of prose, from the most pedestrian to the most lyrical, can be found in the Bible. I won't take for an example one of the great and famous passages from Job or Ecclesiastes, works of which parts, in our Authorized Version, may be described as, and could be printed as, what is called "free verse": I will take, rather, a less well-known passage from the small and neglected Epistle of St. Jude, which is tucked away just behind Revelation:

> Woe unto them!
> For they have gone in the way of Cain
> And run greedily after the error of Balaam for reward,
> And perished in the gainsaying of Core.

These are spots in your feasts of charity when they
  feast with you,
Feeding without fear:
Clouds they are without water
Carried about of winds;
Trees whose fruit withereth,
Without fruit, twice dead,
Plucked up by the roots,
Raging waves of the sea
Foaming out their own shame;
Wandering stars
To whom is reserved
The blackness of darkness for ever.

Again and again here we find repetitions—repetitions
of word, of alliteration, of assonance, of stress, of
phrase length: the passage does not make a regular
pattern, but it makes a pattern with regular elements
in it. Such a progression towards that systematic
symmetrically shaped regularity which we call verse
may be observed in the more exalted utterance, not
merely of great writers, but of the veriest tub-thumper
in the park when excitement or vision is strong upon
him, though his vocabulary be ill-chosen and his
grammar weak.

They say that verse originated with the dance:
what is that but another way of saying that humanity,
when strongly moved, desires regularly rhythmic
expression. Verse is dancing in words. Not all verse
is poetry: once the formula of the pattern had been

found, anything could be put in it: there is even verse which is not poetry, but is nevertheless pleasant, because of its wit, its concision, the deftness of its workmanship. Dr. Johnson, ridiculing the simplicity of the old ballads, improvised the stanza:

> I put my hat upon my head
> And walked into the Strand,
> And there I met another man
> With *his* hat in his hand.

The man who would call that poetry would be a bold man: it is verse; but had verse never just come into existence in response to the demands of the emotions it would not have existed. And even that bald parody gains *something* because it is regular metrical form, with rhymes—which are but one form of repetition, or recurrence, among many. I could repeat the subject-matter in indisputable prose, thus:

> I put my hat on my head, went out into the Strand, and there was another man who was carrying his hat in his hand.

I will repeat it in the Johnsonian form, with the sonority that verse almost automatically calls forth:

> I put my hat upon my head
> And walked into the Strand,
> And there I met another man
> With *his* hat in his hand.

A practising poet would have some criticisms to make of the execution of this. There are too many initial "h's" in that last line for easy recitation, and the stress upon the first "his" is awkward. Yet the fact that the regular form permits of, and even insists on, musical chanting results in a certain stirring effect, quite apart from all the associations that such a quatrain may have for a well-read person, or an old countryman who remembers his father singing the last of the folk-ballads when he was a child. Sir Philip Sidney said that he could never hear the old ballad of Chevy Chase without feeling his heart stirred as it were by a trumpet: there are faint echoes of that trumpet still in that nonsense of Johnson's.

Prose: poetry: verse. Now there is nothing like a concrete example. I take the first passage that meets my eye in my search for raw material, namely the opening of the first leading article in yesterday's *Times*. The second leading article would have suited my purpose better, for it was about the General Election in Norway, and there was an obvious opening for the play of associations, fjords and fells, trolls in the mountains, clear Arctic airs, and wastes of snow. But it is better to stick to the programme, and I take the first. The "leader" begins:

> The inter-party Committee which is examining the problems of Unemployment Insurance is holding a further and probably a decisive meeting to-day.

Since it adjourned three weeks ago, responsible statesmen in all parties have publicly acknowledged the necessity of drastic reforms in a system which all have recognized to be no longer in any sense an insurance system.

Nobody could call that anything but prose, and pretty prosiac prose at that. Now I could convert it into verse without great difficulty. As for instance (the sentiments, this being a political address, must not be taken as mine):

> To-day once more the old Committee meets,
>   Examining the problems of insurance,
> Two million men are still upon the streets,
>   The tax-payer is taxed beyond endurance.
> We're tired of Mr. Snowden's "Pay, pay, pay,"
> Let's hope they'll come to some result to-day.
>
> This body last adjourned three weeks ago,
>   Since when the leaders on all sides have said
> Drastic reforms must come at once, and so
>   We take it that the present system's dead.
> Ours is an age of many a crying scandal,
> But none, we think, to this can hold a candle.

That is undoubted verse. I think the mere conversion into verse, though I made not the slightest attempt at contriving cunning subtleties of melody to get at the reader's feelings, or even at wit, gives the matter a certain "kick." But it is not poetry. No: the man who should be writing poetry about this subject would approach it in a very different way, and his expression, though it would inevitably be rhythmical, would resemble mine not in the least.

I shan't attempt to write poetry, even prose poetry, about a Committee on Unemployment Insurance. But it is a vulgar error to suppose that poetry could not be inspired by it. There is poetry in any object, provided that the observer has eyes to see and happens to be in the right frame of mind when he is looking at it. A man contemplating those two sentences might suddenly think of all the grim realities behind our abstract words like "Committee" and "Unemployment" and "Insurance": seeing the individual man or woman, workless and burdened with a family, or workless and lonely in streets, far away from London, which have never been heard of by anybody who sits on that Committee; and might be struck with awe at the thought that what are regulations and clauses and amendments in Whitehall are agony or relief, hope or despair, life or death to people elsewhere, who may hardly know where Westminster is, but who have been born, and have painfully learnt in childhood what sort of rough world they have been thrown into, and made up their minds to struggle their best, and given hostages to fortune, and been desolated by the prospect of defeat, underserved, and brought, each in the solitude of his own soul, face to face with that problem of evil, of wanton pain and

suffering, which is the torture of the philosophers.
Or a poet might envisage the Committee as men,
fallible men (great names, but no man is ever as great
as a name can be), meditating the weight of their
responsibility, baffled in private, putting a brave face
on it in public, pathetically endeavouring to cope
with issues too great, perhaps, for any human brain
to master. Or he might again, were he more occupied
with the mysteries of all existence than with the
sufferings of one of those generations of men who
are but as the millions of leaves of a season on the
tree of Eternal Life, see that Committee, sitting so
seriously in its room, worrying over its figures and
its distinctions between so-called "deserving cases"
and so-called "work-dodgers," as small and pathetic
figures against the background of the Universe,
tormenting themselves over things which tormented
the Egyptians in their day and the Romans in theirs;
and the Egyptians are gone, and the Romans are gone.
Or he might, were he more detached, at a glimpse
of the committee-room, find an inspiration in a shaft
of sunlight striking a water-bottle, and the mellow
hue of old portraits on the walls, and the hush of an
empty, waiting room, which has grown wise after
seeing so many Committees come and go, but remains
silent. Nothing, nothing, nothing in life is immune
against the poet. There is always a tendency in the
minor poets to become petrified, to find beauty only

where it has been found before, to look at the infinite .
only through accredited windows: and, indeed, owing
to the long chain of old associations, it is much easier
to get a sentimental response out of people by mentioning a ship than by mentioning an aeroplane. Why
am I emphasizing this in a chapter on the Enjoyment
of Words? Why, because in a large measure—and I
have already dealt with some other aspects of the
matter—the enjoyment of words is the enjoyment of
things.

A tome would not suffice for all that even
I could write about poetry and verse: all I can
hope to do in these chapters is to throw out a
few disconnected observations that may possibly
prove suggestive. I shall now make one which has
no obvious relation at all with those which have
gone before: I have not been at the pains to establish
an apparent transition from one paragraph to another.
But it is, I think, an observation which is of importance to those who are seeking to increase the amount
of enjoyment they get out of their reading, but who
may have found particular difficulties with verse. It
is this: When you are in any difficulty, read the thing
aloud, and read it with the accentuation that you
would naturally employ. All the best verse flows
naturally, if spoken in what has been called "speech-
rhythm": anything that does not is not good verse.
The greatest modern master of rhythm was the late

Poet Laureate, Robert Bridges. Often and often people have come to me and told me that they have stumbled over his verses, because they could not make them scan. My reply has invariably been: "My dear idiot, you forget all about scansion; poets never think of it, and never have to think of it. You just read the stuff aloud, and you'll find how perfect the pattern is." I won't take a good example to illustrate my point! I will take a bad one. And a popular one.

According to Dr. Johnson, whom I have already quoted, Sir Robert Walpole, Prime Minister of England, said that at his dinner-table he always talked obscenity, "for in that all could join"—which was very considerate of him. All, I think, can join in Longfellow's *Psalm of Life*. It owes its immense popularity to the fact that it contains a large number of important and salutary truths—truths that are so truthful that they tend to be considered platitudes, and consequently it is not the mode to repeat them, and consequently they may be lost sight of. Not for one moment would I dispute a single thing that is said in that so celebrated poem about our responsibility to a higher power, our duty of resisting pessimism, our obligation to remember that better men than we have found the fight worth fighting; and Longfellow put it all in very simple language that anybody can understand. But he *did* miss something. I must have said over and over again that words, if

we are to enjoy them fully, must be both accurate
and pleasant-sounding. But in verse something more
is demanded: the sentences, as we should naturally
speak them, must not fight with the pattern of the
verse, or we get the feeling that there is something
unnaturally artificial about it all. The first verse of
that excellent *and* execrable poem of Longfellow's
runs thus:

> Tell me not in mournful numbers
> Life is but an empty dream,
> For the soul is dead that slumbers,
> And things are not what they seem.

It is all very encouraging, no doubt. But how have
we read it? Why, with the maddening, unintelligent,
vocal see-sawing of a parcel of village school children
chanting "Twice one is two" on a summer afternoon
when the larks are singing beyond. Were the words
not cramped into that stiff metrical framework, never
would we pronounce them thus. Consider the second
line. It might reasonably be pronounced in several
ways, as, for example,

> Life . . . is but an empty dream,

and with a pause after the "life"; or the stress may
come heavily upon "dream" or even upon "empty."
But say it in whichever reasonable way you like,
another metre appears. And precisely the same thing
appears in the last line, which can only be made to

fit the metrical scheme if a quite unjustifiable weight is put upon the word "are"—a weight that no human being would put upon it in conversation.

Read your poets and pretenders to poetry in the light of that. The recurrent beat makes an impression on its own account, but let it coincide with the natural stress of speech and the effect is far stronger. Good poets know that, and take immense trouble to fit everything in. Bad poets throw out a mechanical tune and some agreeable sentiments, and hope for the best.

V

THE ART OF WRITING

THE Art of Writing—well, these chapters are not meant for professional writers, and the last thing I wish to do is to increase the numbers of professional writers. Goodness knows there are quite enough of them at present: and the few who are very good need no instruction from me or anybody else. Not more than one in twenty of the books which are published survives, even among a few readers, twelve months after it is published; and he would do an ill service to literature, or to the economic situation of a hard-pressed country, who should urge people who had never thought of doing so before to write books. Those who have it in them to write good books will do it without encouragement: what I am thinking of is rather reading than writing.

But the practice of writing, "not necessarily for publication" (as the phrase goes), is a great assistance towards the enjoyment of reading. If we have tried to do a thing ourselves and failed, we can with all the more relish appreciate the work of those who have tried and succeeded. When our ancestors founded the traditional system of classical education in England, and ordained that every miserable little boy should

attempt to write Greek and Latin verses (as, in many
of the schools of England, they attempt to this day),
it was not with the notion of producing a crop of
poets who could write Latin and Greek verses which
could compete with the best works of the ancients:
there were not more than one or two in a century
who did that. The notion was that between the few
geniuses and the mass of complete stupids there was
a large number of boys who through failing, or half
succeeding, to discover their thoughts and feelings
and express them in terse and muscial language, con-
forming to certain rules which were not arbitrary but
the fruit of experience, would all the better understand the achievement of those who had performed
the miracles of which they themselves were incapable.
And by the same token, the practice of writing
English, with a very large number of people, must
sharpen the edge of the enjoyment of reading. If there
is anybody reading this now who has ever tried to
write poetry in secret—but no, that is a very silly
start. I once made a bet with a man that I would
ask the next fifty people I met, *tête-à-tête*, whether
they had ever attempted to write serious verse, and
that every one of them, under pressure and the seal
of confidence, would (as the old journalists used to
say) "admit the soft impeachment." I lost, but I only
lost by one man, who was a civil engineer. Every
kind of unlikely person, sometimes after trying semi-

mendacious evasions, confessed that there had been a moment when poetic success was dreamed of. If they had never attempted it at any other time, they had at least yielded to the temptation of pouring out their intimate feelings when they were young and in love—yes, Cabinet Ministers and M.P.'s of all three parties, and even Professors of Economics. Most of them added to their confession some such phrase as "I don't know what made me do it," or "Of course it was all the most dreadful rot, and I can't imagine why I am telling you." Well, what was true of the first fifty people I catechized in 1919 must be true of thousands and thousands of others: almost everybody attempts to compose something in writing at some time, just as almost everybody at some time or another has attempted to draw a picture, if only a portrait. And what I say to them is this: Don't be ashamed because you are not Shakespeare, and don't be disturbed because you may never write anything fit for publication. If you have time and inclination for it, let words be your hobby. Play about with them in verse or in prose: you may not think of anything worth saying, and if you do you may say it very badly; but the more you experiment, once you have realized the conditions of the job, the better will be your critical sense, and the more pleasure you will get out of the works of the masters. Much that the masters put into their works is missed by most of their readers because they are not looking out for certain things, or perhaps do not even know that they exist. This is so even with very popular authors. A good example is Mr. P. G. Wodehouse—who is the contemporary successor of Mr. W. W. Jacobs— a popular jester who is also a careful and skilful artist. Anybody can enjoy his ingenious and complicated plots, his rough, hearty satire, his charmingly imbecile young men, his terrific fathers and aunts from whom the young men have expectations, his resourceful heroines, his simpletons triumphant and his biters bit: but it is only a minority which gets an additional savour out of the flow of his sentences and the frequent exquisite choice of his words. One may illustrate the same truth from another angle. The most popular poets in every generation are almost always those who tell stories and—in their lifetimes, at least, before the schoolmasters begin using them as texts—the poems in which they tell their stories are much more popular than the poems, equally good or better, in which they do not tell stories. What this means is that although (as I said before) anything is given a little extra "kick" by being expressed in vigorous repetitive rhythm, what is said matters much more to most people than the way in which it is said. For lack of the development of the critical faculty, most readers would as soon read the narrations of Tennyson and Byron, provided the same events happened and the same sentiments were expressed, in bad doggerel as in superb verse. I cannot be the only person who has heard Tennyson's glorious *Revenge* and *Out with the Lifeboat* recited by the same man to the same village audience on the same evening with equal success.

It is somewhere said that nobody expresses himself so well, so forcibly, and so economically as the non-professional with a story; and one does sometimes come across a narrative by a sailor, say, or an engineer which compels one's admiration by the closeness with which words fit things, and by the absence of trivial literary decorations. But the statement that the un-professional write best is only a half-truth—not perhaps as much as that. One does occasionally meet one of these men of action, full of character, blunt, direct, shrewd, who talks well and writes as he talks. But most people write much worse than they talk. The world is full of people whose conversation, taken down by a typist hidden behind a screen, would read excellently—racy prose, no cant, no stale expressions —but who, as soon as they get pen in hand, write in a manner commonplace, or worse than common-place. They aren't used to the medium; they are frightened or awestruck when they see a sheet of white paper in front of them; they at once, being unfamiliar with the technique of writing, cease to be themselves, and start writing stilted and second-hand sentences that never could pass their lips. No journalist ever writes such appalling journalese as the private citizen who, once in a while, sits down, heavy with his consciousness of the solemnity of the occasion and the dignity of print, to write a letter to a local paper. The vast majority of such letters would be infinitely more persuasive, as well as infinitely more amusing, were their authors to write them as nearly as possible as they would speak them to a familiar friend. Think of the sort of thing we see. A gentleman, signing himself "Citizen," "Plain Man," or "Pro Bono Publico," writes to the *Gazette* or the *Sentinel* about Mr. Baldwin or the public drains, and he begins: "Sir, the nature of public feeling on this momentous subject now having been made clear in no uncertain voice," clotting the thing up with bad grammar, woolly comparisons, and phrases which have lost all their force because of incessant mechanical use. In conversation what the man would say is—I naturally eliminate everything that convention rightly prohibits in print—would be something like this (I am dealing now with the local drains, not with imperial politics): "Look here, Mr. Smith knows as well as I do that this disgusting nuisance simply cannot go on." But people won't write as they talk. They feel, when they sit down to write, that they must live up to the majesty of authorship; and their notion of how to secure that is to drag out of memory's wardrobe every moth-eaten royal robe, every blunt halberd, every scrap of tinsel and gilt cardboard that they can lay their hands on: the result being that millions of people, all of them individuals with their own little differences of character, opinion, and speech, all write exactly alike.

I suggest that practice may prevent that, and that practice can be obtained by everybody. No one need write letters to the newspapers. But there isn't one of us who isn't occasionally obliged to write letters to friends or relations. You, my reader (if I may arbitrarily take an example), are going to-morrow to write a letter to your brother, your mother, or your wife. Well, you think that there is nothing to say: that is one mistake, for there is always something to say. If one's object really is to give pleasure to the person at the other end, it can always be given, provided care is taken with one's expression, by describing as vividly and amusingly as possible anything that one may have seen or done during the day. No day in anyone's life is ever exactly like another: if we will only stop and think, and not be lazy about it, there is always something which will move the person at the other end: and, after all, the chief difference between a private letter and a published essay or article is that one is addressed to an audience of one or two and the other to an audience more numerous. But beyond the "matter," there is the manner. Even in letters, even in the letters of the least skilful of us, a difference may be made to the people at the other end, and our own faculties will be sharpened, if we look before we leap, and think before we write. Half the population of England ends its letters with "Hoping that this will find you well as it leaves me." Well, it is a very laudable sentiment, and the first time that the phrase was used it must have seemed rather near and rather touching. But when you have had it at the end of a hundred letters it means no more than "Yours truly" or a full-stop. We cannot all, as I have said, be professional authors; and, as I also said, I am thankful for that. But we are all obliged, since we all learnt to read and write, to be amateur authors; and there isn't a human being who ever writes a letter who hasn't it in his power to give more pleasure at "the other end," and carry more conviction, and even promote his own interests, by considering his thoughts a little before trying to put them into words, and his words a little before finally inscribing them.

What to avoid. Read Sir Arthur Quiller-Couch's book, *The Art of Writing*, read particularly the chapter on "Jargon," and you will discover *some* of the things which should be avoided. You will discover, for instance, that it is really rather silly to say, "This is especially so in the case of Lord Hugh Cecil," who, happily, is not yet in a case at all. But all the things that are to be avoided are implicit in a catalogue of the things that are to be sought. The first thing to be sought is Accuracy.

I am writing—it may be a poem, a novel, an essay, or a mere letter. Call it a letter. I have seen something. Certain aspects of that something struck me with particular force, and inspired in me (if I allowed myself to think) particular thoughts. I must, if I am going to write anything worth writing, first of all discover what I did see, what I did feel, what I did think. Not what others felt and thought before me; not what I suppose that I ought to have seen, felt, and thought. No, what I actually saw, felt, and thought myself. It may be that, when the results of the scrutiny appear, I shall be found to have seen, felt, and thought what thousands before me have seen, felt, and thought, though even if that be so there will inevitably be a slight difference; for no two human beings are precisely alike, as no two leaves on the countless trees of the countless generations of trees have ever been exactly alike. But the only path to salvation as a writer, whether as a public writer or a private writer, is the path of accuracy. Disentangle your own response to what you have observed from all the responses you know about or conjecture. Make sure of what you do yourself see, feel, and think. Then select from your impressions those which are best calculated to convey the picture you wish to convey and produce the effect you wish to produce, remembering always that the concrete image has always more force than the abstract generalization; then, if God has not given you the divine gift of speaking automatically in musical phrase, consider the noise that your words make.

The Art of Life consists in getting all we can out of every experience that we have. Training, as well as natural talent, is required before we can do that. The same thing applies to the Art of Writing. I may say for myself—taking myself purely as a specimen, and not as somebody more interesting than anybody else—that it was only by very gradual stages that I learned what was involved in writing, and attained, in some measure, the ability to say what I really thought in a way that was really my own. When I was very young I wrote poems in the manners of Edgar Allan Poe and Mr. Kipling: I was intoxicated by their tunes, so I took over their opinions and outlooks, kept in two compartments, for they didn't mix very well. When I was a little older I fell under the influence of the French decadents, particularly Baudelaire: that poet wrote so well about despair and corruption that for a time after first encountering him I, too, could write about nothing except mouldering corpses; which didn't interest me in the least, and a despair which, thank God, I never knew then and have never known since, however present daily the thought of death may be to me. I am, I must assert again, taking myself as a specimen. Gradually I discovered that none of these artists, great though may be the debt that I must always, artistically, owe to them, thought in the least like me, and that I had been taking at second-hand opinions that did not fit me in the least. I discarded them. I began to try to express in my own language, though echoes of their melodies may always be present in what I write, what I really saw, felt, and thought—forgive this reiteration—myself. Life is short and Art long: the curtain may come down before I have discovered myself entirely, and learnt to speak in a language entirely concordant with my own nature. But the path of progress is clear enough: and it is one that may be followed, in his own sphere, by everybody, poet or prose-writer, professional or layman. "Don't lie" is the first maxim I would like to ram in, and "Tell the truth with a music that will assist it" is the second. Realize these two things, and those of you who never dream of writing for publication will get greatly increased pleasure out of the works of the great writers: for they will know what the great writers were trying to do.

VI

THE THINGS BEHIND WORDS

I HAVE in the previous chapters, I will not say covered, but at any rate glanced at, various aspects of the enjoyment of words—considered historically, psychologically, phonetically, in regard to their associations and in regard to their relation to musical metrical schemes. But to one truth I have devoted very little attention, and that is that you will not get much enjoyment out of words unless you have developed and retained the capacity for enjoying the things behind them. And that is not so easy. Most adults' capacity for enjoyment is very restricted.

When I refer to "enjoyment," I am not referring to enjoyment through the grosser senses. I have frequently, in public places, heard ladies put enormous relish into requests for "a nice glass of port," and I have heard an audience cheer with sympathetic fervour a music-hall song of which the refrain was "I *do* like an egg with my tea." But the enjoyment of food and drink, though well enough if not carried to an animal excess, is frequently the only enjoyment which people experience in any intense degree. Suppose you are sitting in a restaurant and your companion said, "There's a man behind you who seems to be enjoying

his food," you don't have to turn round to see what
he is like. You will know that sitting there, bent in
awful concentration over a porterhouse steak, will be
a portly man with protruding eyes, flushed cheeks,
distended veins, multiple chins and necks, who has
long ago ceased to enjoy anything except his food.
Invite him to consider the exquisite colour of the spot
of ruby light shining through his uplifted glass of
wine, and he won't know what you are talking about.
Quote to him, "My love is like a red, red rose," and
he will surlily reflect that he doesn't see how a woman
could be like a rose, considering that a woman has
eyes, ears, a nose and a mouth, and a rose has not.
Mention the moon to him, and he will think only of
a round white thing, alleged to move round the
earth, which is sometimes in the sky at night, though
he hasn't noticed it lately; he knows it is always
mentioned in silly, sentimental songs, and may dimly
remember that long ago, when he was still capable
of making love, it used to have an absurdly disturbing
effect upon him. Invite him to consider the fact that
all the hundreds of diners present will be dead within
fifty years, and he will be angry, as though one had
been guilty of indecent exposure of the soul. For him
a million million dawns have broken in vain, and all
the generations of the flowers and the stars beckon
to him fruitlessly; all the graces and all the tragic
beauty of dead civilizations are as nothing to him;

he is unaware of the emotional appeal that lies in the strength of the oak, the fragility of the butterfly, the noise of rain on leaves, the stealth of creeping mist, the passing freshness of youth, the dignity of age; and he walks unseeing daily before the ultimate majesties of Good and Evil, of Life and Death. The sense of wonder has gone: and yet, as a child, he probably had it.

Now there is a good deal of nonsense talked about children. Wordsworth's *Ode* and its "trailing clouds of glory" is often gushingly misapplied; as also its original, that poem of Vaughan's which begins:

> Happy those early days when I
> Shined in my angel infancy.

Children are not angels in every regard; in some ways they are little savages, badly in need of moral (as well as hygienic) education. But the phrase "childish delight" is significant; and it is significant that savages are frequently described as being like children. They share the virtues as well as the vices of children: the pleasure that a savage takes in coloured glass beads (for which he is often laughed at by the people who give them to him in exchange for the rubber and ivory out of which we make our own not necessarily more beautiful toys) is a pleasure that we all of us knew when we were children, and that most of us lose, or severely limit, as we grow up. The contrast is often painful between dull, unimaginative parents, incapable of delight, and their children, who can be ravished by colour and rhythm, to whom each new object that they see is a miracle of shape and contrivance, and who easily and habitually employ the power of visual imagination. R. L. Stevenson said that he was puzzled to know what became of all the horrible medical students and where all the nice doctors came from. In the same manner, one might well be puzzled as to what becomes of all the sprightly children, and where all the heavy grown-ups come from. That is to say, one would be puzzled, did one not know that to some extent the process of degradation has taken place in oneself, and that one is always in danger of losing one's sense of wonder completely.

> Shades of the prison-house begin to close
> About the growing boy.

Surely, whatever compensations we may have had, it has been the experience of almost every one of us that, as we have grown older, our impressions have grown less sharp and our habit of exposing ourselves to them has disappeared. That the whole freshness of a child's awareness should be retained when things have grown familiar cannot, perhaps, be expected. Moreover, we can find all sorts of excuses for the way in which we allow the scales to grow over our eyes, and even over our hearts. Here we may refer to another hackneyed passage in Wordsworth, the sonnet which begins with:

The world is too much with us, late ôr soon,
Getting and spending we lay waste our powers,
Little we see in nature that is ours,
We have given our hearts away, a sordid boon.

(I may remark in parenthesis, once more recommending a close attention whilst reading, that "late or soon" is a very clumsy inversion of a quite unnecessary "sooner or later," and that "a sordid boon" is another piece of padding put in to provide a rhyme for the moon, with which Wordsworth could not bear to dispense.) The truth of statement is unexceptional; and the situation, to some extent, cannot be avoided. It is pardonable not to notice the sunset if you are thinking of your debts, and he would be a monster of detachment who could admire the buff-coloured paper or elegant typography of a demand for unpaid income tax. But the world is with none of us the whole time: we simply let ourselves get out of the habit of really looking at things, and really allowing ourselves to feel them, letting the pageant of life and nature pass before unseeing eyes, refusing emotion because we are too indolent or too drugged in body or in mind. It is easy enough to lapse, but not so easy to get back. I suppose that some of my elder readers may remember the tremendous vogue of Professor Henry Drummond's book, *Natural Law in the Spiritual World*, which was an attempt to construct a biology of the spirit parallel to the biology of the body, with which the Darwinians had startled his generation. I dare say much of it is out-dated now, but there was one truth, perhaps a commonplace, which was very effectively driven home, and that was that there is not one of our faculties, moral, intellectual, aesthetic, which will not atrophy if we neglect to exercise it. Mr. Chesterton once remarked, speaking of mankind's affairs in general, that unless you keep on whitening a whitewashed wall it will go black. You will go "black" unless you retain the resolution not to let yourself get crusted over by custom, not to repeat judgments at second-hand, not, if you still think and feel at all the beauty, richness, and mystery of life, to subsist entirely upon impressions that you received when you were more observant and more discriminating, and allowed your sensibilities to be reached as you do not allow them to be reached now —though you may be unaware that years have passed since you knew the shock of beauty or of strangeness. This last unawareness overcomes far more people than know it. It is a matter of common observation that many writers, even great writers, draw entirely on their childhood for the material of their books, continually devising new variations on the same old themes. It is well enough even to live in the past with a perfect acuteness of enjoyment, even if you have, after certain years, withdrawn into a tower with your secrets, content to experience no more. But it is better still to remain capable of experience: to be perpetually renewing the enjoyment of immediate contact with the world around, and perpetually enlarging the pastures on which memory may feed.

I have just used a word, "experience," which is very much in vogue just now, and which is used with alarming vagueness. Judging from the way some prople talk, one might think that "experience" meant breaking the Ten Commandments, or serving three months as a dustman or a stoker when you had no intention of remaining one. No; these things may be done, and the doer remain precisely the same afterwards as he did before, except that he may have lost an illusion or two which he need never have contracted. There are tiresome persons who imagine that you cannot describe a murder convincingly without committing one. It was of these persons that Disraeli was thinking when he said, in his twenties, that if one had Imagination one did not need Experience. When he was seventy, he was asked if he still was of that opinion, and he said that he was, only more so. Experience, as I am using the term, is a matter of quality of perception and of response, not of mere brute rushing through a variety of physical scenes.

And anything we go through may be experienced with almost any number of degrees of intensity and fullness.

The poets, so long as they remain poets, have this faculty in its fullest development: the great poets retain the child's capacity for wonder and untarnished vision, and couple it with the man's powers of analysis and of intellectual imagination. Some, including some who are of no great general eminence, but conspicuous in this one regard, are "poets all the time," so to speak, never losing the wonder in their eyes or in their words, and being charmingly, if rather pathetically, unable ever to exhibit common sense. But all, until or unless they cease to be poets—as some have ceased—are in frequent exercise of the faculty of wonder or, one might better say, are able frequently to make the surrender to wonder. There is a poem of Mr. de la Mare's called *The Scribe*. The poet imagines himself sitting by a tarn, a little lake in the hills. Well, had his imagination conformed to many people's reality, he might have conceived himself saying, "Well, it's nice and quiet here, well out of the wind. What about that lobster?" proceeding then, though in a manner soothed by the warmth and allayed by the peace of the landscape, to talk about golf handicaps and look at nothing around. But what *does* he write? This:

THE SCRIBE

What lovely things
   Thy hand hath made:
The smooth-plumed bird
   In its emerald shade,
The seed of the grass,
   The speck of stone
Which the wayfaring ant
   Stirs—and hastes on!

Though I should sit
   By some tarn in thy hills,
Using its ink
   As the spirit wills
To write of Earth's wonders,
   Its live, willed things,
Flit would the ages
   On soundless wings
Ere unto Z
   My pen drew nigh;
Leviathan told,
   And the honey-fly:
And still would remain
   My wit to try—
My worn reeds broken,
   The dark tarn dry,
All words forgotten—
   Thou, Lord, and I.

There you have the man who will never allow the cares of life to overwhelm him or the advance of age to ossify him. The nearer he gets to the grave, the more acutely he is aware of the certainty of death, the more he will be anxious to miss nothing of delight in the universe around him; and we can all of us, however heavy the burden of trouble or practical business that lies upon us, however we may at moments sink under it into indifference and callousness, find enough moments of retreat to enjoy everything—the words and the things behind the words— even as he.

And there is a world of enjoyment, in this sense, around us wherever we are. A man of imagination can voyage through all the worlds. Coleridge, in the *Ancient Mariner*, envisaged, in all their dramatic solitude and vastness and simplicity of colour, the wastes of the Antarctic seas. Read that poem, and then conceive what kind of letter a person who had lost his youthful freshness would have written about it all, e.g.: "Dear Mother and Father, It is very cold here, and there is a lot of ice about. Yesterday we saw a bird they call an albatross, and a member of the crew shot it. We had a good wind for some time, but now it has been calm for some time. The sun is redder here than it is in Peebles. We saw a funny sort of ship the other day, I don't know what it was. We are running short of water: this was very careless of the agents." You may go where you like, and miss everything; you may stay at home and, failing the pleasure of travel, imagine much (with a little basis of information) about the ends of the earth. But romance, for all the spell that strange names and colours and plants and climates have over us, is not to be found only in far places. Beauty is at our doors —and every day. Tennyson illustrated this in his poem about the "Flower in the crannied wall," which contained all the secrets of all life. But I will take a more present illustration. I will take the wireless.

Ten years ago this invention was in its infancy. Everybody said, "Isn't it wonderful what these scientists do? What will they be doing next?" Now everybody takes it for granted, and the chief interest that many have is to criticize the programmes adversely. Now I am not taking the wireless as an example because it is a new development of science or more remarkable than anything else; for that matter, the reception of vision by the brain through the eye that responds to waves in the ether, like any wireless set, is equally awe-inspiring. I am taking the wireless as an example simply because it is, at this moment, very present both to you and to me.

Imagine I am broadcasting. You are there, ten, or a hundred, or a thousand miles away. I am here, with a water-bottle and a chaste little square microphone in front of me, in a sort of artistic padded cell; I read these words, and they go forth, and you hear them, and they go forth beyond you, possibly sending reverberations into farthest space and farthest time, imperceptibly echoing for ever into an outer limbo where are eternally preserved all the sights and sounds of the remotest ages. But the voice is less important than the person: forget the machine, remember the communication: remember that what you hear over the wireless are not disembodied voices mechanically making sounds, but instruments—our voices are instruments though made of flesh—played by spirits who are here for a season and then will be gone, calling to other spirits across the deep, surrounded by all the other deeps. In other words, don't get used to things: if one thinks things have gone stale, it is oneself that has gone stale.

"Si jeunesse savait, si vieillesse pouvait . . ."—"If youth but knew, if age but could. . . ." It is bound to be always true, this sad dichotomy of practical affairs: youth cannot believe the world to be what it is, and age, when it has realized truth, has no longer the energy to act on it. But in our present connection, with an effort, as we grow older, we can combine the advantages of both states: youth cannot anticipate the wisdom of age (though, if it will, it can take some of it on trust), but age can, if the spirit is sufficiently vigorous and faith sufficiently alive, keep burning the enthusiasm of youth without its delusions. I adjure you, difficult though it may be, and many though may be the temptations to sloth, to keep your eyes clear, though that may involve effort, and to keep your heart open, though that may involve suffering.

I will say another thing about the enjoyment of words—this time not directly from the aesthetic or emotional but from the intellectual point of view—though, in the last resort, the pleasures of the intellect are emotional and aesthetic also. It is this. Don't let words become shibboleths to you. Life will be much more interesting to you, and you will be much more interesting to other people, if you do not.

When Mr. Baldwin first became Prime Minister, one of his first actions was to go down to the Cambridge Union and inform all the aspiring undergraduate orators that "Rhetoric is the harlot of the arts." This is true; though in a world where spellbinding is bound to be done the answer is (in the old phrase) that "it is better not to let the devil have all the best tunes." Speech is, in large measure, used for persuasion; the arts, not merely of rhetoric, can be used to enforce persuasion; genuine passion earns its influence if simulated passion does not.

Spell-bind others, if you like, by the force of your eloquence and the passion of your conviction; yield, if you will, to the same thing in others; but don't allow words to get an hypnotic influence over you when you have never really examined the things behind them.

I will take instances (I am not going to be controversial) from the vocabulary of politics. I know people who foam at the mouth if one breathes a word in favour of "aristocracy" as a method of government; I know others who are equally indignant if a favourable allusion is made to "democracy." To one side "aristocracy" means the greedy tyranny of an unqualified few; to the other "democracy" means the drab dictatorship of an ignorant many. To him who detaches himself, and considers the literal meaning of words and the course of human history, these terms merely connote alternative systems of governing a country, each of which may be better than the other in a particular place and time (morality not being involved at all), and each of which, in any particular circumstances, must be judged by its capacity for making everybody happy as far as possible. "Liberty," "Free Trade," "Protection," all these words, with many people, are used as armour against thought: come down on whichever side you will, but do consider, when using these abstract terms, what they really mean, not only to you, but to others, and what they have meant in the past. The believer in aristocracy is no good if he has never considered the dreams of the great democrats, and the obscure hankerings of the speechless mass; the believer in democracy has not begun to think if he supposes that the mere word carries its own conclusive arguments with it.

Expose yourself to the essences of things, and

think, when you have leisure to think, of the meaning of words, especially those words which you habitually use as though they were arguments. So will all life be enriched and illuminated for you. If only I could feel that these chapters had done anybody else as much good as they have done me, I should be a very happy man indeed. But for that matter I am.

PART TWO

THE ENJOYMENT
OF LITERARY FORMS

I

POETRY

THESE chapters, of necessity, can contain little more than a few facts and suggestions which may be useful to the ordinary reader of books. I shall avoid the technical terms of the prosodists, their anapaests, amphibrachs, and hendecasyllabics. A knowledge of prosody is no more necessary to the reader who wants to enjoy poetry than a knowledge of physiology is necessary to the spectator at a football match. I would lay long odds that not a quarter of the poets I have known could have explained what an amphibrach was.

As much applies to forms. There are people who love to talk of "rondeaus" and "villanelles" and "ballades"—the last a form still copiously practised. These forms are amusing to poets: though none so much as what Wordsworth called "the sonnet's narrow plot of ground." It is fun to take a set form and see what one can do with it: all the more so in that all men work better within rules. But let not the diffident be too worried about these things, or even about the difference between blank verse and rhyme. Milton, in his preface to *Paradise Lost* (though he had done lovely things in rhyme), attacked rhyme.

But rhyme is only one more kind of repetition; and it is the repetitiveness of the rhythm that distinguishes verse from prose. Enjoy yourselves with poetry: do not be distracted by arguments as to the superiority of this, that, or the other method of expression. Emotion engenders regular rhythm: to regular rhythm we can all respond. Some poets employ it to convey conceptions which few (for lack of education or intelligence or imagination) can take in, and others employ it (in Keats's phrase) to express what all men feel but cannot say. Take what you can from it: do not suppose that what you cannot understand is nonsense; and believe that the poets are the flowers on humanity's tree. "They learn in suffering what they teach in song"; they welcome Pain in order to sing; if you are deaf to them, consider it your fault not theirs. The poets are those who are habitually on the highest plane to which the ordinary individual reaches.

Do not be side-tracked by critical disputes. There is always a good deal of talk among critics about movements and schools in poetry, and a certain number of poets, not usually good ones, announce that they intend to demonstrate new theories and create new forms. Those who really do create new forms usually say very little about them, and new theories as to the nature and function of poetry are hardly likely to be valid at this time of day. The best

known "school" in the history of English literature
is the so-called "Lake School of Poets," and Wordsworth, Coleridge, and Southey had very little in
common except that they happened to be friends in
youth, and were agreed that the poetry (like other
things) of the day needed humanizing, and that the
diction of eighteenth-century poetry had become too
stilted and too removed from ordinary speech. This
was quite true; but nobody could have supposed that
Kubla Khan was written by Wordsworth; and the
better poetry of both sprang from the same sources
and dealt with the same subjects as all the best poetry
in the world. In our own day you sometimes see
allusions to a "Georgian School." They never called
themselves that; they were merely a certain number
of younger poets, selections from whom are gathered
together in a series of volumes by Mr. Edward Marsh,
an anthologist of genius. But they had very little in
common (except what they had in common with the
general tendencies of their day), and many of them
thought each other no good at all. For some years
after the war the place teemed with groups of young
people who labelled themselves with all sorts of
"isms," on the Paris model—the French delighting
in schools and movements, being a nation devoted
to ideas, a prose nation rather than a poetical nation.
Some of them were very extreme indeed, though
none so extreme as the French Dadaists, who printed

things upside-down, and sometimes composed poems which consisted of rows of exclamation and question marks of varying length. Stunts come and go: the man who thinks that a new technique makes a new poetry is confusing the means with the end. Sir Philip Sidney said the essential word on the subject when he said, "Look in thy heart and write."

The greatest poetry arises out of a state of emotional and imaginative excitement. Wordsworth defined poetry as "emotion recollected in tranquillity." It is often quoted, but it is only true of some poetry. The great lyrists, such as Catullus, Heine, and Burns, probably poured out their songs when they were at white heat of emotion. We know that Tennyson's "Break, break, break," one of the most affecting and inevitable lyrics in English, welled straight out of him when he was walking alone within sound of the sea and thinking of a friend who was dead. Consider it, and consider how simple are the elements of it:

> Break, break, break,
>   On thy cold grey stones, O sea,
> And I would that my tongue could utter
>   The thoughts that arise in me.

> O well for the fisherman's boy
>   That he shouts with his sister at play!
> O well for the sailor lad,
>   That he sings in his boat on the bay!

And the stately ships go on,
  To the haven under the hill,
But Oh for the touch of a vanished hand,
  And the sound of a voice that is still.

Break, break, break,
  On thy cold grey stones, O sea,
And I would that my tongue could utter
  The thoughts that arise in me.

In point of fact, Tennyson's heart uttered those thoughts much better through not uttering them. A diplomatist once said that language was given to conceal our thoughts: it is certain that it can never entirely reveal them. But we do an immense amount by suggestion and by intonation. Anybody who is not too petrified to forget what it is to be in love will remember how much can be conveyed by such simple ejaculations as "Darling!" "Oh!" "Yes," and "No, no," and what different meanings according to the way in which they are spoken. The poet who has mastery over his metre compels his reader (provided the reader surrenders sufficiently, forgetting mechanical beats, as to read the lines in the natural intonation of speech) to speak his lines with an emphasis and an inflection which convey things unspoken, compelling a rush of excitement or a sigh, with all its implications.

I do not think that examination of a good poem by

people who have not been moved by it is likely to do much good; but there is intellectual fun in examining a poem which actually has moved one. Let us go through this most spontaneous and simple of all lyrics. "It is art to conceal art," the old saying goes; but if you have a genuine poet writing impulsively, he gets with ease precisely the same results as the most consummate artist will get in cold blood. If Virgil, who wrote twelve lines a day and no more, had considered that first line, he would probably have come to the conclusion that the best way of indicating the recurrent wash of the waves on the shore was by that triple reiteration "Break, break, break." You will notice that at the beginning and the end of the word there are strong syllables; they mark the divisions, the pauses between the waves, and the determined quality of their arrival: "wash, wash, wash," or "roll, roll, roll," or "fade, fade, fade," would have produced quite different effects. The "break, break" is like the ticking of a clock— the sea's clock; and, feeling it rather than thinking of it, the mere sound reminds us of the inexorable passage of time which takes all hands away from us and stills all voices. In the next line the long "o" in "cold" concentrates attention on the longevity of the ocean as opposed to the short duration of man; and the long "a," for that is what it really is, in "grey" reinforces the impression. There is a failing at the end of the word "utter" which indicates human incapacity to cope with the immensities of the universe; there is a duration and stress on "arise" which reflects the struggle of the human spirit to cope with them.

Tennyson might, had he not been in an excited condition and imaginatively awaked, have passed a hundred times the fisherman's boy playing with his sisters. In that awakened condition, the imagination, not the laborious reason, at once selected from among the hundred sights and sounds around him that one image of the innocent children at play, unaware of time and death, so violent a contrast to his friend who had died. In the next stanza the contrast is pointed. The traffic of the world continues: the loved one has gone. And then, almost automatically, he returns to his main theme, and we are reminded again of the eternities and of man's unanswered questions that are addressed to them.

That is an example of a purely spontaneous poem, drawn out from a man in a state of emotion, who could not but speak music when in that state. Shakespeare says:

> The lunatic, the lover and the poet
> Are of imagination all compact.

And when the poet or the lover is at the point of lunacy (provided he has a vocabulary) there is no question of art concealing art: the soul governs the tongue, and the tongue speaks music. Few men remain long in, or enter often, that divinely inspired state in which the god seizes them by the hair and the tongues of Pentecost descend. Most poetry, even most great poetry, though the bones of it may have originally been stirred to life by the breath of the visionary Muse, is in large part deliberate: art has to work out an approximation to what inspiration would have dictated had it been in action. Consider, in contrast to the poem I have just quoted, Tennyson's "Blow, bugle, blow." Or consider such a lyric as Robert Bridges's (from his marvellous *Shorter Poems*), April 1885:

Wanton with long delay the gay spring leaping cometh;
  The blackthorn starreth now his bough on the eve of
    May:
All day in the sweet box tree the bee for pleasure
    hummeth:
  The cuckoo sends afloat his note on the air all day.

Now dewy nights again and rain in gentle shower
  At root of tree and flower have quenched the winter's
    drouth:
On high the hot sun smiles, and banks of cloud uptower
  In bulging heads that crowd for miles the dazzling
    south.

That would be a pleasant thing, for it represents pleasant things, to anyone even who had not an ear;

much pleasanter to one with an ear. But if this last, having succumbed to the music, had also intellectual curiosity, he would find that the poet, without parading what he was doing, had employed assonance, alliteration, and internal rhyme to almost an un-paralleled extent. "Wanton" and "long" have the same vowel sound; "delay" and "gay" in the first line anticipate the "May" of the second; there is hardly a vowel, hardly an initial consonant which is echoed in an effective place. The poet began by loving an April day; but his poem does not gush out: it is an exquisite contrivance in which all the concealed artifices lie hidden to be discovered by the explorer.

It remains emotional, and full of the sense of mystery. A good deal of the most interesting work written by English poets is neither emotional nor mysterious. There are those who strive after a definition of the differences between poetry and verse: so do not I, recognizing that almost every-body who has written poetry has lapsed into verse (which, if well written, may make the most common-place statements more amusing and epigrammatic), and that there is scarcely a writer of verse who has not occasionally, perhaps because of the mere in-vigorating quality of the tom-tom beat of verse, soared into poetry. It is better not to bother too much about the differences between the two. Leave that to the experts who can write neither poetry nor verse. The thing is to enjoy these quintessential comments on human life, and, if you cannot enjoy all of them, to enjoy those of them which suit you. "In the house of poetry are many mansions," said Leigh Hunt, who had been a friend of Byron, Shelley, and Keats, all of them as different as men could be, but different kinds of men heightened to a common degree of expression. Keats dreamed of physical and sensuous beauty; Shelley dreamed of the perfectibility of man and of imaginary worlds where people more perfect than men roamed free from all men's limitations; Byron was a man of this world, acutely conscious of those limitations and of his own, who was sceptical about all the dreams of his time (though, like all poets, he, too, hankered after Paradise), and spent a great deal of his time writing verses which were epigrams in which observation of life was qualified by a sense of how much worse it was than it might be, and by a wit which took delight in the compressed description of its drawbacks. Those were all poets of one "romantic" generation: there were centuries of poets behind them, all, according to their ages, different from them.

Take what you can from any poet. Probably only the poets, who are very few in each generation and a kind of secret society at that, can take everything from each other that is offered: there are indeed (it is a conventional expression) "poets' poets," the full enjoyment of whom is granted to be the privilege of other poets, and some of whom seem quite dull to even very intelligent persons who are not sensitive to the last fine shades of terminology or of rhythm. There are, on the other hand, persons with a gift for deft versification who remain on the humdrum plane all their lives, but can give an aesthetic delight because of their talent with the instrument. Those are few who can enjoy everything from Chaucer to Spenser, from Spenser to Pope, from Pope to Calverley; he who cannot should take from poetry what he can, and be willing to admit that his inability to enjoy what he cannot is his misfortune and not somebody else's fault.

II

THE ESSAY

THE word "essay" is an intimidating one to the vast
majority of the British population. It carries with it
memories of efforts at school to compose one or two
laborious pages on "How I Spent my Holidays," or
"Which would you rather be, a Sailor or a Soldier?"
It has, by the same token, painful associations for me.
The first piece of really careful prose I ever remember
writing was composed for a school essay on "Egypt."
I thought of the Sphinx and the Pyramids, of Philae
and the Valley of the Kings, of the Pharaohs going
back into the mists of remote antiquity; I thought of
the ancient Nile, rising in the mysterious Mountains
of the Moon and flowing past all those monuments
now, when they are crumbling, as of old when they
were bright and new; and I laid myself out to write
Ruskinian paragraphs full of colour and cadence, in
which the words "illimitable" and "eternal" occurred
much more frequently than I should allow them to
occur now. "Well," thought I to myself complacently,
"I can't imagine that anybody else has done anything
like that." Did I get a prize? No; I wasn't even
commended. All that happened was that I was taken
aside by a master, who knitted his brows and bit his

lips, and asked from what author I had copied out
the passage on which I had dwelt most lovingly—the
passage fullest of the venerable river, the immemorial
sands, and the brooding spirit of antiquity. When I
denied that I had copied it from anybody, I was
invited to consider the old maxim that "lying only
makes the offence worse," and I ended by narrowly
escaping a beating for having the germs of a poet
in me. This by the way; but I was trying to write
one type of essay when another type was wanted.
I was expected to write: "Egypt is a very old country.
There was once a ruler there, a very wicked man
called Pharaoh, who was drowned in the Red Sea
for persecuting the Jews. The chief sights of
Egypt are the Pyramids, which are not all the
same size, and the Sphinx, which is a very large
Sphinx."

Well, we are not talking about school essays. Nor
are we talking about scientific, religious, political,
and economic essays. Malthus wrote an *Essay on
Population*; probably at this moment somebody is
writing an *Essay on the most advantageous use of
Phosphate Manures in Metalliferous Areas*. The word
"essay," in English, covers a multitude if not of sins
at least of painstaking dullnesses. But when one talks
of "The English Essay," one does not think of these
or even of critical essays, however excellent, like
Matthew Arnold's or Walter Bagehot's, but of a

particular kind of wandering, personal thing which has flourished in England as nowhere else.

It didn't begin in England. Its father was indisputably Montaigne, the quiet French seigneur who lived in his castle tower in Gascony and allowed his mind to wander where it would over life and history and books, without caring whether or for how long he digressed, and exposing (even, one might say, for the public delectation, exploiting) his own character in order that others should see their own reflections in it. That, I think, indicates one of the things that draws people to the English essayists when they are most typically English essayists. They have all rambled into the descriptive and the informative: we owe to Hazlitt a marvellous description of a prize-fight and first-hand impressions of the Lake Poets; we owe to Lamb inestimable portraits of the old actors and the old Benchers. But even in those essays they contrive to be very personal, and their most quintessential essays—and Lamb is the most quintessential of all essayists—are purely personal. When we are reading a novel, the last thing we want to be reminded of is the existence and peculiarities of the author: the author must be forgotten in the story. But when we are reading an essay, the more personality we get the better, whether it be that part of personality which consists of the qualities common to all men (and we are all comforted by being told that the great, whether writers or otherwise, share our weaknesses, hankerings, tastes, affections, fears, and prejudices) or whether it be that part which is peculiarly individual. The typical English essayist is an attractive and charming person who gives us conversation (his statements not being made on oath) such as we might have at an ideal dinner-table, only polished and refined as verbal conversation never can be.

Now the first of the great English essayists was Francis Bacon. He would certainly never have written had it not been for Montaigne, but this great lawyer and scientific man who was going to become Lord Chancellor never acquired Montaigne's gift of personal confession. For all his vast curiosity and sense of history, he could never quite give himself away. Take two instances. First, the beginning of his celebrated essay, *Of Gardens*:

> God Almighty first planted a garden; and, indeed, it is the purest of human pleasures; it is the greatest refreshment to the spirits of man; without which buildings and palaces are but gross handiworks: and a man shall ever see, that, when ages grow to civility and elegancy, men come to build stately, sooner than to garden finely; as if gardening were the greater perfection. I do hold it in the royal order of a garden, there ought to be gardens for all the months of the year, in which, severally, things of beauty may then be in season.

And later that most famous sentence from the *Essay on Death*: "Men fear Death as children fear to go into the dark." You may deduce from it, if you will, the fact that Bacon, in this regard, shared the dread of his fellows; but he doesn't say so, he remains detached, unwilling to confide except by implication. His essays are marvels of concision, wonderful repositories of worldly wisdom and observation, full of sudden magics of vocabulary and sound. But they do not establish an intimacy between writer and reader; and the typical English essay is the much more confidential work of a much more modest man.

The first English essayist in the modern sense was Abraham Cowley, whose essays (though in print at the Oxford University Press) are at the present time as neglected as his ingenious and, occasionally, lovely poems. "Who now reads Cowley?" asked Pope, more than two hundred years ago. The question might still be asked, but all the time he had had a few affectionate lovers. Listen to this, written in the middle of the seventeenth century—the beginning of an essay which at once shows Cowley's consciousness of whence his essays derived and forecasts the whole tone of the English essay from his day onward. It comes from his essay, *On Greatness*.

> Since we cannot attain to greatness, says the Sieur de Montaigne, let us have our revenge by railing at it: this he spoke but in jest. I believe he desired it

no more than I do, and had less reason, for he enjoyed so plentiful and honourable a fortune in a most excellent country, as allowed him all the real conveniences of it, separated and purged from the incommodities. If I were but in his condition, I should think it hard measure, without being convinced of any crime, to be sequestered from it, and made one of the principal officers of state. But the reader may think that what I now say is of small authority, because I never was, nor ever shall be, put to the trial; I can therefore only make my protestation.

> If ever I more riches did desire
> Than cleanliness and quiet do require;
> If e'er ambition did my fancy cheat,
> With any wish so mean as to be great,
> Continue, Heaven, still from me to remove
> The humble blessings of that life I love.

I know very many men will despise, and some pity me, for this humour, as a poor-spirited fellow; but I am content, and, like Horace, thank God for being so. . . . I confess I love littleness almost in all things. A little convenient estate, a little cheerful house, a little company, and a very little feast; and if I were ever to fall in love again (which is a great passion, and therefore I hope I have done with it), it would be, I think, with prettiness rather than with majestical beauty.

Honesty and whimsicality—and confidential button-holing: there are all the things here that make people love Charles Lamb. The pedigree is straight from that to Hazlitt's *On Going a Journey*:

> The soul of a journey is liberty, perfect liberty, to think, feel, do just as one pleases. We go a journey chiefly to be free of all impediments and of all inconveniences; to leave ourselves behind, much more to get rid of others. It is because I want a little breathing-space to muse on indifferent matters ... that I absent myself from the town for a while, without feeling at a loss the moment I am left by myself. Instead of a friend in a post-chaise or in a Tilbury, to exchange good things with, and vary the same stale topics over again, for once let me have a truce with impertinence. Give me the clear blue sky over my head, and the green turf beneath my feet, a winding road before me, and a three hours' march to dinner—and then to thinking!

I may be doing a few people a service if I recommend a perusal of the essays of Abraham Cowley.

Since him, what a procession! There are obscurer men whom I might mention. I should like to send readers back to the neglected essays of Alexander Smith, whose *The Lark Ascending* (you may know his poem *Barbara* in the Oxford Book) is one of the most beautiful and thoughtful essays in English. But Addison, Steele, Johnson, Lamb, Hazlitt—it would require hours to celebrate adequately their contributions to our enjoyment. And in our own day Mr. Beerbohm, Mr. Lynd, Mr. Knox, Mr. Belloc, Mr.

Lucas, Mr. Chesterton have continued the old tradition. We may regret that they mostly write so briefly: that cannot be helped; a contributor to periodicals has to write to the length required. All these authors would doubtless pour themselves out much more fully and ingeniously were they invited to write at Charles Lamb's length, and we may regret that (with the exception of Mr. Beerbohm) they do not. But it is agreeable to see spirit triumphing over matter, and posterity will take pleasure in the spectacle of men of letters of our own day continuing to compress their effusions within the limits of a newspaper column and still keep their freshness, their humour, their sense of beauty, and their capacity for exposing themselves as specimens of mankind. The reader of, for example, Mr. Belloc's *Hills and the Sea* forgets, after he has read it, that the essays are so much shorter than the essays of old; he merely remembers that he has shared one man's delight in life, laughed with one man, loved the beauty of the earth and sea with one man, dwelt in awe with one man, and enjoyed much prose, still noble, although written for a quite contemporary and very likely commercial press.

III

THE NOVEL

WHAT is a novel? I suppose the answer of the ordinary readers of novels would be, if he (or should I not say she?) were asked, would be that a novel is a story long enough to fill a good-sized book. I think that, for our present purpose, we had better accept that rough definition. The sophistical analyst might suggest that there was no intrinsic difference between a story in prose and a story in verse. Certainly, if you think of the subject-matter and the way in which it is treated, the *Odyssey* of Homer is a picaresque, or rambling, novel in verse very much akin to *Robinson Crusoe*, and Chaucer's *Canterbury Tales* has a great affinity to Mr. Priestley's *The Good Companions*—a very great affinity indeed. Chaucer's people, the Wife of Bath, the Pardoner, the Knight, the Clerk of Oxenforde, and the others are brought together from all the quarters of the country to embark on a common enterprise, and we are told all the stories of their various pasts, and, incidentally, as the relevant backgrounds are successively introduced, presented with a picture of England in Edward III's day such as we could never construct from legal, constitutional, or economic documents. While we are reading the

Canterbury Tales we are enchanted by the music of the verse: weeks afterwards, we have forgotten that, and remember the characters, and their humours, and the colour of the time. I may remark, in parenthesis merely, that those poets are usually most immediately popular who, like Lord Byron, Sir Walter Scott, and Mr. Masefield, tell stories in verse, adding the magic of metre to narratives of the kind which, in prose, most appeal to their time. However, we cannot discuss poetry here.

Another person who might quarrel with our definition is the learned historian. He might point out that the word "novel" derived from a foreign word which was used of a short story. The Renaissance Italians wrote short stories which they called *novelli*—from one such collection Shakespeare drew freely for his plots. He got, for instance, the plot of *Othello* from a so-called Italian "novel." It handicapped him. In the original, Othello is a rather unattractive character who conspires with Iago to kill his wife by letting the canopy of her bed collapse upon her, apparently by accident, and is then blackmailed by Iago. This, I may say, handicapped Shakespeare. There is a story in one of Sir Arthur Quiller-Couch's books of a sailor at Portsmouth who went to see *Othello* acted, and, at a critical moment, shouted out, "You great black fool, can't you see!" What happened was that Shakespeare took over the old plot, that when he began writing, Othello, in his shaping imagination, became a very intelligent and sympathetic and unselfish man, and that the man (who would have been much more liable, in the circumstances, to have killed himself rather than the woman he loved) had to be made to fit the old plot. But I am wandering again. However, the point has been made that what we are talking about is the novel as we would now define it, and not earlier literary productions to which the name has been applied. The novel, to us, is a work in prose, and a work which is of such a length that we cannot call it a short story.

It is common form to say that *Robinson Crusoe* was the first novel. This is not true. The late Greeks had their novels: the *Daphnis and Chloe* of Longus is certainly a novel. The Greek novels are novels of episode and event rather than of character; the heroines may be seized ever so often by pirates, but no seizure ever brings out any new point in their characters. Novels, nevertheless, they remain, if only early precursors of the *Treasure Island* school. The *Golden Ass* of Apuleius is a novel: the hero is turned into a donkey and goes through the most surprising experiences, in respectable households and amongst brigands, and we are given a very vivid and amusing panorama of ancient life while the tale is being told. The *Satyricon* of Petronius—supposed to have been the Beau Brummel of Nero's day—is a novel. It is, in

parts, a very squalid novel; but it is almost Dickensian
in its mixture of comedy and tragedy, in its miscel-
laneous portraiture, in the vividness of its shifting
scene, in which we can recover the life of the time as
it was led by all types of persons, including the newly
rich and the inhabitants of the underworld, male and
female. The Elizabethan romances—I recommend
The Unfortunate Traveller of Nashe, but hardly dare
recommend the verbose *Euphues* of Lyly—are novels
of a kind; the French romances of the seventeenth
century, though intolerably long and tedious and
insufferably highly pitched, are novels; and what is
Don Quixote but a novel? *Don Quixote* was a novel
—a century earlier than *Robinson Crusoe*—which was
written partly in order to expose the false sentiment
of a whole school of earlier novels, romances of
chivalry which the author thought were too remote
from ordinary life. As he went on Cervantes fell in
love with his hero and the chivalric ideal; long before
we reach the end we feel that a lunatic who tilts at
windmills is a more attractive person than a wholly
sensible man who never tilts at anything; and, while
following the fortunes of Don Quixote, we have
obtained such a picture of the Spain of his day as we
never could have got from the historians.

The novel did not begin with *Robinson Crusoe*. But
it is true that the multiplication of novels dates from
Robinson Crusoe's time. It was in the eighteenth

century that women, in England, began to read on a large scale; and the more women have read the more the novel has become dominant. With the appearance of the novel of the moment, women authors—who had only occasionally dipped into poetry and scholarship—began to get more numerous. Aphra Behn and Mrs. Manly were among the first professional novelists, and love, of one kind or another, was their normal theme. Had literature remained male, we should have had our few great novelists perhaps, and our shocker-writers, but not the innumerable tribe who are chiefly preoccupied with the relations between men and women. But most men like facts: history, biography, numismatics, travel; and the modern novel is chiefly a supply to a demand from women, who either want to learn about life in an easy way or wish to escape from life in a romantic way. I repeat again: we cannot regret it. The development of the novel has given us Jane Austen and Fanny Burney, Scott, Dickens, Thackeray, Trollope, Meredith, and Hardy, each of which last was also a poet. It is fascinating to watch the evolution of the form. Experiments in method are continually made. Nobody knows where the novel may go next. But it *is* important to remember that a story is a story, and not necessarily a story having any real relation to life at all.

Two pieces of advice I may give to intelligent readers of contemporary fiction. The first is: that if

you really want to read the best, do not rush at new
books. If you want to read six new novels a week,
well and good: you are the mainstay of the publishing
trade. You will easily find, in the reviewing columns
of the newspapers, six new novels a week which are
hailed as masterpieces: read them, and forget them.
But if you only want to read the good (though,
occasionally, you may find that some critic upon
whom you rely really convinces you that a new book
really is a masterpiece), wait a little. The "book of
the season" is very seldom the book of the next
season. It is talked of for a month or two, and then
it is forgotten. But if somebody intelligent tells you
to read a novel a year after it has been published,
there is probably something in it. Remember that the
reputations of most of the great novelists have been
made slowly—Hardy and Conrad are recent examples
of this. The people who get the immediate success
are the people who appeal to the fleeting taste of the
day, and who deliberately appeal to it. They do not
love anything; they do not sit down and endeavour
to present a vision of life as they honestly see it;
they do not care about the permanent elements in
human life. They think about the moment as much
as any milliner with her hats: the vogue passes and
"the place of them knoweth them no more." A study
of the files of any literary newspaper for the last
hundred years would be a melancholy study: we

should continually be encountering "great" novelists now completely forgotten. It is difficult, perhaps, to realize that oblivion will be the fate of most of the so-called "great" novelists of our own day, but it will be. There is Mr. A, who has relied mainly on shocking the suburbs and the provinces by painting alarming pictures of the life alleged to be led by the fast, smart set in metropolitan London. There is Mr. B, who is, intrinsically, a journalist, and who makes his appeal by painting pictures, essentially trivial, so realistic that everybody gives a shout of recognition when he sees them. There is Mr. C, who represents in himself the typical religious or political mood of the time, and writes novels in which the characters have precisely the doubts and ideas which are momentarily most common amongst those people who have doubts at all or ideas at all. But yesterday's doubts and ideas are not to-day's doubts and ideas. Your true novelist or dramatist takes all these things in his stride, is not greatly influenced by contemporary movements, and concentrates on the permanent elements in human nature. Your Chaucer, your Shakespeare, and your Cervantes are far more modern than your out-of-date novelist of 1896 who was championing some cause now so finally won or so hopelessly lost as to be no longer interesting. Think of Grant Allen's *The Woman Who Did*. It made a vast sensation in its day, shocking all the Victorian

notions of propriety. But where is it now? Gone, one
might gloomily say, with the propriety. And still
Hamlet wonders about Life, Death, and the Eternal,
and still Lear raves upon his heath, and still Macbeth
is egged on by his woman to do a deed of which his
conscience will never approve.

That is one thing: the novel of the year is very
seldom the novel of next year. Another thing is this:
do not think, in a general way, that you will learn
anything about how to conduct your life from novels.
A few of the greatest novelists—most of them poets
at heart—have put into their novels all they knew of
life, in a conscientious way; from these, possibly,
something may be learnt, and certainly in good fiction
we can get the general panorama of life as we can
get it nowhere else. But most novels (however
realistic in superficial aspect) are (so far as their
central themes are concerned) written by born
romantics who are not writing about anything they
have known and seen, but about life as they wish it
would be, or hope it is, or fear that it might be.
How many governesses in the novels of the late Mr.
Charles Garvice married dukes and earls disguised as
clerks or tramps? But how many have done it in
real life? This gift of making vivid pictures is a
dangerous one: "this must have happened," we think
as we read; but it never did. By the same token, the
most violent and hectic novels are usually written by

the tamest people. "Out of the strong cometh forth sweetness" is the Biblical text. Beware of novelists who offer you scathing exposures, the "burning core of life," audacity, defiance, flaying, and so forth: they are usually working off the inferiority complex. Thomas Hardy and Joseph Conrad, both of whom I knew, were strong men and courteous gentlemen: in their writings utterly truthful and restrained, in person quite undemonstrative. There is a tendency, in this age of print and of conflicting philosophies, to think that ferocity on paper implies strength of character. It doesn't.

IV

THE PLAY

Not long ago an eminent living dramatist informed a newspaper reporter that, although very successful in the theatre, he had the greatest contempt for it. The person who drew my attention to the statement was rather shocked by it; but I wasn't. The author in question had obviously been maddened by two things: the limitations of the theatre, and the ease with which, quite cold-bloodedly, he could secure effects in the theatre. He had the same sort of revulsion against the theatre as a popular orator might have against big political meetings, a skilful demagogue who knows that he has only to get on a platform and say certain things, meant or not meant, and the whole audience will cheer, laugh, or weep. The theatre and the drama, in other words, are peculiar.

The most obvious peculiarity about the drama is the tiny portion of it which survives its own day. In other departments of literature there is a constant accumulation: there are so many good books in the world, still living, still read, still written about, that seventy years is not long enough to read them in. If you are interested in poetry or fiction, you are always hearing of alleged masterpieces in Finnish, Polish, and Lithuanian which you will never probably have time to read. But if you are interested in the drama, it is quite another matter. It takes no time at all to read all the classics, and when you have read them you may, if you are a curious antiquary, read thousands of other plays which were alive in their day and stone dead now; but if you only wish to read plays which still have life in them, and still appear good, you are very short of pasture.

How few there are! The dramas of the great Greeks, Aeschylus, Sophocles, Euripides, and Aristophanes, still retain their eminence and their readers, and are still occasionally acted. Their numbers may before long be added to if, as Signor Mussolini hopes (he told me so himself, so you may take this as gospel), the new Italian excavations at Herculaneum result in the discovery of lost classical manuscripts. Nearly two thousand five hundred years have passed since those plays were written. What others since them are still, I won't say acted, but even read for pleasure as distinguished from erudition? Virtually nothing (unless one makes an exception in favour of *Everyman*) until you come to the Elizabethans, and then only the plays of Shakespeare and a very few outstanding works by Marlowe, Jonson, Webster, and Beaumont and Fletcher. You have since them a few Spanish plays, Racine, Corneille, Molière, and Beaumarchais in France, and in England a few comedies by Congreve and his contemporaries, by Goldsmith and Sheridan, and by Wilde. You have Ibsen's plays, and those of other moderns who may last. For hundreds of years thousands of playwrights have been turning out plays, many of them enormously successful in their own day, which have now no life in them, and which nobody will ever attempt to revive again, except (in a few instances) scholarly societies, at the universities and elsewhere, who revive demoded plays out of mere curiosity.

Why is this? It is partly because a man who is writing a play to last must have several qualities not commonly found together. The first requisite of a play is that it shall hold the audience all the time; and this applies as much to *Charley's Aunt* as to *Hamlet*. A political speaker or lecturer is done for once his audience has begun coughing; a playwright is done for if for but five minutes his audience begins to think, "How boring and unreal all this is." With a novel or an epic weak patches and faulty construction do not matter so much. The subject-matter and the language are the dominant things; and we will plough through or skim all sorts of improbable, dull, or distended chapters because we know we are going, from time to time, to encounter beautiful or profound things. In the plays that survive the centuries there is beauty and profundity; but no amount of intellect or poetic feeling is of avail if the play is badly made. A playwright has but three hours, and from twelve to eighteen thousand words—the number of words in a long short story—to do his work in. In that space and in that time he must develop his characters and tell his story. He must amuse, interest, or thrill all the time, and all the time (particularly at the end of each act) he must make people keen to know what is going to happen next. If, at the end of an act, they either feel quite certain what is going to happen next, or do not care what is going to happen next, they will probably walk out of the theatre, or, at any rate, only stay there because they have paid for their seats. If this requirement is not met, nothing else is of any avail. Since the Elizabethans almost all the great poets have written plays, or tried to; and not one of them has held the stage, except Dryden (who condescended to the stage) for a time. Coleridge tried, Wordsworth tried, Tennyson and Browning tried: they had immeasurably more brains and passions than most of the successful playwrights of their respective days, but they failed as playwrights because they did not pay sufficient attention to the carpentry side of play-writing. Tennyson's *Becket* was the best of his plays; Henry Irving's acting made it run for a hundred nights or so, but it will never really hold the stage. It was roughly contemporaneous with *Charley's Aunt* —not to mention Gilbert and Sullivan. *Charley's Aunt* is revived annually in London, and runs continually in the provinces. Nobody was ever ravished by the beauty of any scene in *Charley's Aunt*. Nobody ever learnt anything about life from *Charley's Aunt*. Nobody ever came away from *Charley's Aunt* thinking, "I have just heard original thought and powerful sentiment expressed in impressive language." Nobody has ever come away from *Charley's Aunt* thinking (though there are some pretty good phrases in it), "How witty are the epigrams in this play!" And nobody ever came away from the play thinking he had learned something about human nature—which he might have done from one of the outrageously unsuccessful plays of the late Henry James. Yet the characters are sufficiently indicated to be amusing, the satire (though not profound) is adequate, the wit (though not equal to Congreve's) is not so feeble as to "put one off," and all the time there is situation after situation, surprise after surprise, with a little sentimental plot mingled with all the robust humour and shooting one with the second barrel. That play, I frankly admit, I can see again and again. For the strange thing about suspense and surprise in the theatre is that one still gets them, if the play is properly made, even when one has seen the play before and knows precisely what is going to happen.

All the brains in the world and all the heart in the world and all the honeyed speech in the world are of no avail in the theatre, unless technique (which the disappointed call tricks) is good. The author must know precisely how to arrest an audience's attention at the start and how to hold it thenceforward. He must gradually work up to an inevitable climax. However enthusiastic he may be about his theme, he cannot just preach from it. The characters must say what they, roughly, might say; and they must not make speeches so long that the audience suddenly begins to lose its illusion of reality, because nobody (except for a rare philosophical Scotchman) ever makes such long speeches in life. The working out of the plot necessitates the perpetual removal of characters from, and then introduction to, the stage. The amateur playwright gets them on and off by awkward and obvious devices: somebody calling about a dog or a cigarette case left behind. The moment the audience sees through the device and begins to think that the person would not have come on or gone off naturally, but is being dragged about for the author's convenience, the illusion of reality (which we get even in a good, preposterous farce) has gone, and we no longer surrender to the play, we are merely looking at something made up by the author. Readers may be commended to the plays of Ibsen—and particularly *Rosmersholm*—for examples of perfect technique. You may be irritated by his characters and you may be, occasionally, depressed by his subjects and his atmosphere; but his manipulation of a subject with an eye to presentation in the theatre has never been excelled.

"What, never? No, never!"—as they say in *Pinafore*. That doesn't mean that he was the greatest of all dramatists. The greatest of all dramatists, as also the greatest of all poets and the most understanding of all men, was undoubtedly William Shakespeare—of whom we know so little that people are perpetually suggesting fresh members of the Elizabethan House of Lords as candidates for his throne. There is nothing in any play which Shakespeare has not done better, more dexterously, or more dashingly. He knew every trick: he knew, by sheer, uncanny instinct, a great many tricks that nobody before him had practised. He played upon his audiences with every shade of day and night: nobody was more dexterous than he with the tolling of bells and the striking of clocks. But he was hurried; his audiences were uncritical; and he was never so slipshod as not to be able to get his hearers back by something magnificent. The best constructed play of Shakespeare is probably *Coriolanus*. *King Lear* and *As You Like It* run it close. Any modern "play-doctor" (an American phrase) could improve any of them: he was really very lazy. But the "play-doctors" might cut out the good with the bad. They have their rules. You must have action. You mustn't have long speeches. Shakespeare, when at the top of his form, broke all their rules. Witness the play *Richard II*. There is very little action in it. The interest centres in a series of recitations by that fascinating, though decadent, king. His recitations are so full of music and of personality that we want him to go on speaking for ever. All the rules that are made for common men are broken in this play, and the ordinary manager would turn it down on the soliloquies, but it fascinates one, all the same. It doesn't, in fact, matter how you hold the audience as long as you *do* hold it.

But you may hold a contemporary audience and not hold a later one. Shakespeare would never have held anybody had he not had a gift for the theatre; but he would not hold us now had he not had something over and above that—and the same thing applies to the ancient Greeks. One year, in a competent play, a joke about the Indian Conference might bring down the house; or just bring in a dwarf and let somebody call him Carnera, fifty years hence dons will be writing footnotes explaining who Carnera was, just as, to-day, they write elaborate footnotes explaining the exhibits at Ben Jonson's *Bartholomew Fair*. Shakespeare had his topical allusions; nobody knows how many, though they are always arguing about it. But the reason that he is still the most compelling dramatist in the world, for all the careless technique that he mixed up with the consummate technique, is that his main preoccupation was not with the topical but with the eternal. Take any of the great speches, and you will find that they will hit you as hard as they might have hit any of his contemporaries. "To be or not to be," "To-morrow and to-morrow," "How sweet the moonlight sleeps upon this bank"— not only are they completely free from the colour of a fleeting age, not only do they cry across the centuries our common humanity, but they are even phrased as a poet of our own day might phrase them. Fashions change and systems alter, but the human heart does not change.

He wrote in verse mostly. So, it may be observed, have most of the dramatists (except for a few comedy writers) whose works have long survived. The point should be noted. Verse in the theatre is, at the moment, out of fashion. The reason probably is that modern poets who write for the theatre think more about the verse than about the theatre. Shakespeare wrote great speeches: so will they. Shakespeare used images: so will they. Tennyson's *Queen Mary*, with its archaic dialogue of citizens, with its great description copied from Shakespeare's description of Cleopatra, is a warning; that great poet was thinking, not of an audience in the theatre, but of the language of a mighty predecessor. Poetry—and the language of poetry is language of the heart and the imagination at their highest pitch of excitement—will never come back to the theatre until the poets realize they are writing for the theatre and not for the study. On the other hand, the theatre will never be healthy until the poets come back to it. But will the managers know who are the poets? Probably not!

V

BIOGRAPHY

THE passion for reading and writing biographies is a comparatively modern one. Beyond those immortal short lives of Plutarch's the ancients have left us very little first-class biographical writing, though a host of the anecdotes in which they so delighted. They took, as a rule, more interest in characteristics than in character: eccentricities make good anecdotes; the Greeks and Latins, on the whole, lacked our curiosity as to fine shades of sensibility and motive: they preferred the dramatic to the analytic. There is one Greek figure whom we know intimately in his everyday habits and speech. That is Socrates. Read Plato's *Symposium*, read the account of the philosopher's death, and read one or two of the Dialogues, and you are left feeling that you know the old man as well as you know Dr. Johnson. Plato, in a sense, was as much a dramatist as a philosopher: his happy accident has led to our priceless possession of a speaking portrait of the subtlest and most invulnerable talker who ever lived. There is one other portrait of a philosopher, or pseudo-philosopher, which is much less widely familiar. I suppose that if I suggest that you should read the *Life of Apollonius of Tyana* by Philostratus, many of those who have not had a classical training may jump to the conclusion that it is something terrifyingly out-of-the-way and calls for great erudition in the reader. It is nothing of the sort. It is one of the most amusing and easily readable books conceivable. It dates from that period of the Roman Empire when official traditional religion had broken down, and society toyed with every sort of exotic and quack religion, magic, and pseudo-mysticism, and Apollonius of Tyana, a wandering vegetarian and wit, who was now with the Egyptian philosophers, now with the Assyrians, now with the Indians, was just the sort of figure to appeal to it. He is a fascinating character: half-genuine, half-charlatan, picturesque of speech, most impudently witty, a man who said to emperors and kings impertinent things that nobody else would have dared to say. There is published by the Oxford Press a quite perfect translation of the book by the late Professor Phillimore. Anybody who takes the trouble to get hold of it will make the acquaintance of a personality just as amusing as Samuel Butler or Mr. Bernard Shaw, and having a good deal in common with both of them. The one other outstanding biographical work from ancient times is, I suppose, *The Confessions of Saint Augustine*, the prime parent of all books of intimate self-analysis and self-exposure, a work of the most passionate honesty and noble eloquence. The descent is straight from that to the *Confessions* of Rousseau, to Newman's *Apologia*, to Amiel's *Journal*, and to the *Journal of Marie Bashkirtseff*—all those frank self-revelations in which men and women have bared themselves either in order to justify themselves or out of vanity.

The medievals were no more addicted to elaborate biography than the ancients. The chroniclers would roughly sketch a man's character and appearance and record a few typical deeds and sayings, but they never spent years accumulating material about him. It wasn't wholly, I dare say, that they were more interested in large events than in individual people, or that they preferred romance to reality: to some extent, it may be presumed that the absence of the printing press and the prevalence of illiteracy made a difference. Where all copies of books had to be written out by hand—slow in the making and slow in the reading— there was a natural tendency to concentrate on works with a general appeal. A really hearty modern library subscriber can devour, or at least skim, a book a day, which means that he has time to read even incompetent lives of unimportant people. Our own age has honoured the members of Charles II's harem with far more elaborate biographies than the medievals ever compiled for such great figures as Edward the First and Edward III. Moreover, since printing, reading, and writing became widespread, materials are much more easily accessible for full biographies. Edward, the Black Prince, may have made as many speeches as his present namesake and successor; but there were no shorthand writers to take them down and no newspapers to report them. The absence of a postal system made letters few, and people had not the idea of hoarding documents because they might be of interest to posterity. The invention of printing made a profound difference; so did the Renaissance, which enormously stimulated the antiquarian and historical sense. In the Tudor age we have excellent little lives of Wolsey and Thomas More, and in James the First's day we begin to get monographs on the lives of statesmen and even collections of correspondence.

But still the interest is centred on affairs rather than on personality, and the man of affairs is deemed more interesting than the man of thought, feeling, or even action who has no great position in the political world. We know immeasurably more about the Burghleys and the Walsinghams than about any of the poets of the time, who to us, as persons, would be immeasurably more interesting. Interest in the analysis of passion and motive was manifested in the theatre before it affected the historical kind of writing. It was not until the eighteenth century that the big, would-be-exhaustive *Life* in several volumes began to appear.

Nobody can complain of a shortage of biographies now. Almost every Victorian or Edwardian politician who strutted his little hour as Chancellor of the Duchy of Lancaster or First Commissioner of Works has duly received his massive tombstone in two or more volumes. These countless modern large biographies vary in quality according to the competence of the authors and the qualities of the subjects. The best of them all, to my mind, is the Buckle and Monypenny *Disraeli*, now obtainable in a two-volume edition. The writing is excellent. The pages teem with living people, and the central figure, who combined the characteristics of the wit and the poet with those of the statesman (much to the bewilderment of Mr. Gladstone and millions of other serious people), is fascinating throughout, and speaks a great deal in his own vivacious person. Nor are the pages unduly over-loaded with the dull details of dead political disputes such as encumber most of these works. I cannot say as much for Lord Morley's *Life of Gladstone*, which has always seemed to me greatly over-praised, a book heavy with unimportant detail, ill-proportioned, and throwing very little illumination upon the very obscure personality of its hero. We seem in our own time to have evolved a new system in biography. If these huge books can be justified at all, they can be justified as works of reference, as quarries. For a century laborious "official" biographers have been piling these vast repositories of facts on our groaning shelves; now a new race of biographers has arisen who use these things as mines, and produce short and summary books which aim at giving vivid portraits by selecting only salient features. Mr. Lytton Strachey, with his *Eminent Victorians* and *Queen Victoria*, was the pioneer of the method and its ablest practitioner thus far. It has its danger. If an author wishes to behave like an advocate, he can, with a sufficient bulk of material to select from, demonstrate almost any dead person, in a short and cunning biography, to be either very foolish or very wise, either very crooked or very straight. Nothing can be more agreeable than Mr. Strachey's concise and witty portraits and his coloured re-creations of departed scenes. But, when some imitator having neither wit nor vision thinks he is vying with Mr. Strachey by pert cheap scores off the dead, presumptuous familiarity with the great, impertinent assumption of insight, and the piling up of bogus picturesque details, even the most devastating dullness would come as a relief. The Strachey infection has spread widely, particularly in America. I think the worst case I have come across was a "smart" American *Life* of Longfellow. Longfellow may not have been a great poet, but he was a scholar and a gentleman, and he certainly did not deserve to be called Henry all the time by a patronizing modern puppy with no talents at all. However, Mr.

Guedalla, Mr. Osbert Burdett, and M. André Maurois
have used the method very delightfully.

What are the best biographies in English? There
are many charming short *Lives*: there are Johnson's
Lives of the Poets—very entertaining reading; there
are Walton's *Lives* of Donne and others. "So near
and yet so far"—it is a pity that no contemporary
thought of writing a life of Shakespeare, of whom all
we know, personally, is that (according to Ben
Jonson) he was high-spirited at table to such a degree
that he sometimes had to be (by Ben Jonson) sat
upon. I take it that the four best biographies in
English are Boswell's *Life of Johnson*, Lockhart's
Life of Scott, Forster's *Life of Dickens*, and Mr. E. V.
Lucas's *Life of Charles Lamb*. The first three were
written by persons intimate with, and junior to, their
subjects; the last was written, almost a century after
the subject's death, by a devoted admirer who was
gifted with an almost uncanny sympathy with his
hero, and pieced together all the significant letters and
stories so skilfully and revealingly that even a man
who had known Charles Lamb could not have done
it better. If only Mr. Lucas had been in Boswell's
position! Boswell is the greatest biographer in the
language, because he had the finest subject possible
and was so devoted that, after any evening's conversation, he went straight home and wrote down all
that he could remember of it. We must be eternally

grateful to him for recording so much of Johnson's conversation: we are closer to Dr. Johnson, as he lived and moved and talked, than we are to any other dead man; even Lockhart's Scott and Forster's Dickens are dim figures compared with him. Yet there is some truth in Macaulay's contention that Boswell was a fool. Often and often in that *Life* we find that "a gentleman present" makes an asinine remark and is crushed by Johnson, and we know that the "gentleman" is Boswell. He was so devoted, he so enormously admired Johnson's powers of repartee, that he deliberately invited crushing remarks in order to go home and write them down. Johnson, encountered outside Boswell, is not quite such a bear as he appears in Boswell. Many of his rudest remarks were made to Boswell, and Boswell invited them: Johnson, in a general way, did not talk intolerantly, and he was especially popular with women, who never can bear rudeness and find it difficult to pardon slovenliness. Had Boswell been a little more intelligent, the greatest of all biographies might have been even greater than it is. However, we ought not to look a gift horse in the mouth, and here was an almost grovelling admirer of a great man recording for our benefit, *verbatim ac literatim*, countless remarks made by his hero. I wished, just now, that Mr. Lucas had been in Boswell's place. Ought I not rather to have wished that a Boswell had been a companion of Shakespeare's? Imagine it! There

was a Mermaid Tavern. We know from a poet of the
day that entracing tales were told there and jests
made that "set the table in a roar"; but we have none
of the tales and none of the jests. The Elizabethans
were very trying people. They took an immense
interest in the past, but they never thought of
posterity. That, perhaps, is an exaggeration.

> Not marble, nor the gilded monuments
> Of princes shall outlive this powerful rhyme,

wrote Shakespeare; and that was not the only passage
in which he expressed his confidence in the durability
of his verse. But it never seemed to occur to him, or
to his poetical contemporaries, that posterity might
like to know something about their personalities, apart
from their works; and the result is that the biographers
of Shakespeare, painfully delving in the Record Office,
present us with the picture of a man chiefly occupied
with loans and mortgages—which is absurd.

I may, in conclusion, since we are supposed to be
concerned with the enjoyment of what we have and
not with lamentations over what we have not, recommend one or two biographies which I have enjoyed
and which many have not. I suppose it is hardly
necessary to mention the *Father and Son* of the late
Sir Edmund Gosse, but his short *Life of Swinburne*
is a model biography. Trelawny's autobiographical
Adventures of a Younger Son is much less well known:

half of it lies, but what glorious lies! Where I do feel sure that I am recommending something neglected is when I mention Burdy's *Life of Skelton*, which the Oxford Press reprinted some years ago. To say that it is a short life of an eighteenth-century Irish parson is inadequate. But I can truly say that anyone who can enjoy Boswell could enjoy Burdy, and anyone who can love Dr. Johnson could love Dr. Skelton.

VI

CRITICISM

"CRITICISM": it is simply a derivation from a Greek word and means "judgment"—or, better still perhaps, "judging."

The first thing that should be realized about critics is that there are all sorts of them. I frankly confess that the sort that I most value are those who have the ability to perceive, amongst the welter of bad and ephemeral and ephemerally good books, those which will have some sort of permanent appeal. Of such was Leigh Hunt. He never said anything very important about any book or author, but he had the instinctive feeling for the good: he said, "In the house of poetry are many mansions"; he had no bias, and, so far as I am aware, he never missed a good thing— though occasionally he may have deplored the fact that some obviously great author's opinions did not agree with his own.

There is a saying that "the critics are never right." This is a half-truth. There are always some critics who are right. Those who write biographies of great writers and delve about for early reviews of their first books can usually find preposterous commentaries on them. "Truly we are the children, and wisdom was born with us": it is very refreshing to think that our ancestors made great mistakes which we should not have made ourselves. Critics are much the same in all ages. Mistakes are being made at this moment by persons with great reputations. A hundred years hence the critics of our day will look just as foolish as the critics of a hundred years ago do to us. All the fashionable authors will have disappeared, or almost all; all the exciting novelties will have become old, and exploded, eccentricities. One more generation of critics will be derided as persons who gloated over the lead and the silver and missed the gold.

Critics quarrel amongst themselves to-day. They would not quarrel so much if they would only realize that they approach their subjects from all sorts of different aspects and are fulfilling all kinds of different functions. The most numerous class of practising critics to-day are the reviewers in the daily and weekly papers. Now, what is their job, or what are their jobs? At least one, and at most two. At least, since the book is a new book and nobody knows anything about it, their job is to expose the nature of the book, indicate the talents of the author, and, by copious and representative quotation, show enough of the author's style and habit of mind as to indicate to the reader whether he or she would like the book. And, at most, it is their business to convey at once the topical appeal of a book and its prospects of a permanent appeal. Those who certainly do no job at all are those who air their own theories all the time without remembering the hungry sheep who look up and are not fed. It is a very common fault. Often and often I see quite long reviews of new volumes of verse even (in which the matter of execution must be paramount) containing not a single quotation. The job of a reviewer of contemporary work, particularly verse, is to select the most characteristic passages, good or bad, and write his review round them; not to start some argument of his own and then find passages to illustrate it. The late John Freeman, a very good poet and an excellent critic, said that all you could say about anything in the last resort was, "This is good," or "This is bad."

If that were so, most critics would be out of work. For most critics—practising critics—are more occupied with commenting on works whose goodness or badness has long ago been determined than they are with committing themselves to opinions about the new. There are the academic and editorial critics: the people who take works (as it might be the works of Shakespeare) which are indubitably established as classics and write incidental notes about them. Many of the English literature professors (though by no means all) come into this class: they know nothing about contemporary literature, and, if they did turn their attention to it, they would probably fall into the grossest errors, either because of a propensity for the derivative thing which reminded them of the masterpieces of the past, or because of some kink about subject or meaning, or bias for or against some explicit or implicit doctrine in the author.

And there are the philosophic, historical, and scientific critics. These are interested in ideas: in the evolution of theories about this world and the next, in the relation between the works of great writers (poets being the special victims) and the trend of events and opinions in their times, in the reflections, in the works of the masters, of actual material history. These people are very often very informative. They can tell us far more about Milton's spiritual ancestry than Milton ever knew; far more about the evolution of the sonnet than Shakespeare ever knew; far more about the influence of Rousseau on Wordsworth and Shelley than either of those poets were ever aware of. Critics of this historical and philosophic kind are not to be underrated: there is very great interest in the development and conflict of human ideas, religious and political, and the poets are very sensitive recorders. But it is possible to be a tenth-rate author and have very sound, or at least very interesting, ideas; I dare say Martin Tupper was orthodox and sensible to a degree. But it is also possible to be a first-rate writer and have totally impracticable ideas, or none, very definitely, at all. It is also possible not to know what your ideas are: books have been written about the religion of Tennyson and the religion of Browning which would have told those two gentlemen a great deal that they did not know before.

My advice to anyone who reads books is this: do not be frightened by critics or their reputations. Great critics are rare: Dryden, Johnson, and Arnold are amongst the number. Discerning critics of contemporary literature are rarer still: they exist, in some numbers, in private life, but there is never any reason to suppose that the majority of them will both wish to pursue the practice of journalism and have the knack of it. The ordinary newspaper, in this age, as in every other age in which there were newspapers, demands readability first; and your wit and your phrase-maker is very often a bad judge of literature, or, if not a bad judge, cares much more for his witticisms and his phrases than he does for truth. Test your man, in the papers, by your own reactions; decide whether you think about the books he recommends what he thinks; and if you feel, on mature consideration, that you are right and he is wrong, throw him over! The mere fact that a man is allowed to sign columns in a newspaper does not necessarily mean that he is a wiser judge of literature than his fellows: it may merely mean that he is pushing, or knows people, or has a gift of flashy phraseology that makes him widely read.

I think that most of the best critics I have known have never published a line; and that most of that most have been timid about their own opinions. For myself, though I can read my Wallace and my Oppenheim with the rest of them, I confess that I am chiefly interested in the literature which I think may last. Not for ever, perhaps. What is ever? They say that after certain millions of years the earth will go cold, and all our strivings, and all our dreams, the League of Nations, the vine, the nightingale, the rose, will be occluded by deep drifts of final snow. But we have to take these things relatively. By common consent of mankind those things are great which are still readable after hundreds of years; and, for myself, I am content to regard as the best of critics the man who can single out from the welter of contemporary books those few which, long years after we are all dead, will still appeal to that minority of men and women who are content to find consolation and refreshment in the works of the dead. That angle and that approach are not common; those who take that angle and that approach, realizing that this year's fashion in books is like this year's fashion in hats, that fleeting innovations of technique matter not at all when related to the eternal movements of the heart, that the last triumphs of art are simple and not complicated, and that, in the last resort, all human life (whatever its mechanical appurtenances) is limited by the same conditions and surrounded by the same mysteries, read books in the only way possible to a genuine critic or judge. But, over and above all that sense, they must have a feeling for the accuracy of words, and an ear for music—which conveys more than any words can ever convey. Can it be wondered at that critics are few?

However, as a professional and a fallible critic, I ask for pardon for what mistakes I have made, both of commission and of omission. We have our bright moments; occasionally we are drugged by the great spate of books which pours from the press; sometimes, relieved by the symptoms of intelligence in a book, we over-praise; sometimes, dulled by drudgery, we under-praise. The infallible critic would be inhuman.